What Suze Orman Isn't Telling You

Can you AFFORD to repeat your parents' mistakes?

Jonda K. Lowe

JondaKnows, Inc. • Jacksonville, Fla.

This publication contains the opinions and ideas of its author. It is intended to provide educational material on the subjects addressed in the publication. It is sold with the understanding that the author and publisher are not engaged in the business of rendering tax and/or legal advice. The author and publisher specifically disclaim all responsibility for any liability, loss or risk, personal or otherwise, which is incurred as a consequence, directly or indirectly, of the use and application of any of the contents of this book.

Published by JondaKnows, Inc., Jacksonville, Fla.

Cover photography by Eric M. Sullivan

Printed in the United States of America

ISBN: 978-0-692-33082-1

Visit www.jondaknows.com for more information.

This book is dedicated to my father, John E. McComas, Jr., my biggest fan, and to my clients, friends and strategic partners for your loyalty and support through the years.

"Reasonable people adapt themselves to the world. Unreasonable people attempt to adapt the world to themselves. All progress, therefore, depends on unreasonable people."

— *George Bernard Shaw*

TABLE OF CONTENTS

Foreword

In today's world, it's difficult to know who to believe. When it comes to your money, along with your life and retirement planning, we tend to just follow others. Why is that? I think it's simple. We're afraid to make a mistake and you just follow the masses because there is so much information coming at you.

I urge you to read this book. Take control of your life. Make decisions that YOU want to make. Monitor those decisions. Life has a lot of curve balls. Be prepared. Understand expenses, understand the risk, understand the need for liquidity. Be prudent. Know what you have. Know where you are going!

I first met Jonda Lowe three years ago. The person I met was focused, determined, and highly skilled. From that moment, nothing has changed. She first mentioned her desire to write and explain to others the concept of individually designed, overfunded indexed universal life to me over a year ago. She went to work developing how an indexed universal life policy, properly designed can be both a successful asset builder and provide a legacy. I was amazed at her research and commitment.

Fact is, Jonda knows.

She knows the general public is tired of finding their "fix" by following an "ABC" book by others. While they may do well with book sales, Jonda realizes that each person's situation is unique, and that there is no "one perfect design for everyone" and that each individual should consult their life insurance professional and/or investment advisor who has been properly trained.

Jonda knows that most people simply procrastinate about their life and retirement planning. We tend to not ask ourselves the tough questions when we don't have a clear understanding of the possible answers.

She knows that each individual should be treated fairly and that each person should understand the value of the product that they purchase and know the options that are available.

Jonda also knows that after she designs a plan for her client, the work is just beginning. Life is not a perfect walk. Jonda knows that life provides no guarantees and that life happens. She is one of those professionals that realizes a plan will need to be reworked on an occasional basis.

After reading this book, I believe you will agree with me that Jonda knows!

The first step, after reading this book, is taking the time to sit down and review where you've been, where you are, and where you are going.

I've always believed that the first step in building strong assets is a foundation of risk management. Jonda's process provides for that. Understanding interest rates, crediting rates, and expenses is the next key. Next, look at your tax situation. Do you believe that taxes are really going to go down? Prepare for the future, now! Don't just follow the crowd, take control of your finances. Take control of your life. Life is short. Have fun. Develop a systemic formula to provide you an opportunity to live life the way you imagined. It takes control. It takes discipline.

Jonda provides you a "real world" look at how YOU can take back your finances and develop a roadmap for success. Choose your own direction. Begin your journey today.

Danny Rasberry, CLU, ChFC, Rasberry Producer Group

Acknowledgements

This book would not have been possible without the support of my sons, Eric M. Sullivan and B. Wesley Sullivan, and my business partner, Danny Rasberry.

My gratitude also goes out to my parents; Loretta Steel, supervisor at First Bank Ceredo; Mary Beth Wafer, manager, Smith Barney; Rick Lehrer, supervisor, ING.

All of these are key people who molded me, took a chance on me, believed in me.

Preface

Why This Book Needed to Be Written

The single largest segment of the U.S. population (our baby boomers) is staring down the barrel of retirement and, they are not ready. Boomers have had 40-plus years to plan for this day, yet most are coming up short — and by more than a little bit!

But the last 40 or so years have been some of the best years in history to save for retirement, right? Heck, 40 years ago, most large companies still offered pension plans. That was the life!

As of the writing of this book, we are in the 56th month of a bull market. The S&P 500 has increased 163% from 676.53 to 1,782, an all—time high, yet Fox Business reports in a 2013 article titled "401(k): Pass or Fail" that only 22% of workers 55 or older have $250,000 saved for retirement. Is that enough? Absolutely not. Think about this: Even if you get to keep every dime of that $250,000 (which you don't) and you want only $2,000 per month to live on, your money will be gone in a little over 10 years. Are you planning to die at age 75? Not if you have anything to say about it, right? Life expectancy for a male age 65 is 84 and 87 for a female. Yikes!

So how did we get into such a financial mess? Let's take a quick journey back through those golden years. In 1974, the Individual Retirement Account, better known as the IRA, was introduced, allowing individuals who were not covered by a qualified plan at work to save $1,500 annually and receive a tax-deduction for doing so. Yippee!

In 1978, the section of the Internal Revenue Code that made

401(k) plans possible was enacted. By 1980, those plans were beginning to take off, allowing employees to save an additional $7,000 per year provided their contribution did not exceed 25% of their income.

In 1981, those younger than 70½ could contribute to an IRA whether they were covered by a qualified plan at work or not, AND they could open an IRA for a non-working spouse and contribute $250 for him or her as well. In 1982, the maximum contribution was increased from $1,500 to $2,000. Hey-hey, now we're talking!

Aug. 12, 1982, marked the beginning of a bull market that would run until Aug. 25, 1987. The S&P 500 increased 228.81%. Four short months later, on Dec. 4, 1987, we entered into another bull market that would extend to March 24, 2000, and drive the S&P 500 up 582.15%.

While all that was going on, IRA contribution limits remained unchanged at $2,000 per year. A new type of IRA known as the Roth IRA was introduced in 1997 that allowed investors to forego their tax deduction on their contribution in exchange for receiving tax-free income during retirement. Wow! Now investors had a choice. They could contribute to an IRA, a Roth IRA or a combination of the two so long as their total contribution did not exceed the annual limit. This was all in addition to the contribution they could make into their company-sponsored 401(k) plan, where the annual limit had increased to $10,500. And don't forget the company match! Think about that. If you and your spouse were both working and contributing the maximum to your 401(k) plus max funding Roth IRAs, you were saving $25,000 per year at a time when the market was red hot. Retirement, here we come!

Financial advisors were popping up everywhere. According to the Bureau of Labor Statistics, the number of financial planners in the United States rose to 94,000 in the year 2000, financial advisor/author/TV host Suze Orman released her first book and Y2K went off without a hitch. What could go wrong?

On March 24, 2000, we entered a bear market that would last 18 months. Another one started Jan. 4, 2002, that would run for nine more years.

I was sitting in my office that Monday morning of 9/11 when the news of the towers being hit came across my screen. We were now smack-dab in the middle of what would turn out to be three years of back-to-back losses for the S&P 500. Never in the history of the stock market had we experienced anything like this ... down 10.14%, then 13.04% and another 23.37%. Before it was over, investors had lost anywhere from 40%-60% of their portfolios, depending upon how aggressive they had been.

Not to worry. We can fix this — so we thought. To help investors get back on track, IRA and 401(k) contribution limits were increased to $3,000 and $11,000 respectively. A "catch-up" provision was established allowing those 50 or older to contribute an additional $500 to the IRA of their choice and $1,000 to their 401(k). During the next 60 months, the market would return a total of 101.50%, repairing most of the damage.

But you know the rest of the story (we love and miss you, Paul Harvey!). Just when we thought we saw light at the end of the tunnel, Lehman Brothers filed bankruptcy, banks began to fail, the United States Credit Rating was downgraded and for the first time ever, stocks and bonds were down at the same time. There was no place to escape. By the time this financial crisis was over in 2009, the markets had given back 57%.

As I think about the financial morass we as investors are in, I have to ask myself, could this have been avoided? If the tech bubble had never burst, if the towers had never been hit, if the housing market had never crashed ... and on and on. I'm not really concerned about what happened. There will always be a crisis. I am more concerned with whether we have had the best information available to us in order to make the best decisions. I believe the answer to that question is a resounding "no."

With access to more than 330,000 securities, commodities and financial services sales agents, nearly 8,000 mutual funds, financial gurus on every other channel, a plethora of books on investing and the Internet, why can't we get this right?

The answer is we — and I do include financial advisors,

insurance agents and financial gurus — refuse to stand up and think. Have you ever seen an ad for a "no-load" mutual fund? You probably have. By definition, "no-load" means the shares are sold without a commission. From that definition, many, if not all, owners of these funds believe they are free. If they are free, who paid for the ad you saw in Money magazine? Is the fog starting to clear? I don't care if it is Fidelity, Charles Schwab or Charlie Brown, nobody works for free! That no-load ad you saw was paid for by YOU, the investor. Are you surprised? You shouldn't be. Financial companies are in the business to make money.

With that in mind, I have resolved to find real answers, challenging everything I have been taught by the financial services industry. What I discovered was more than disturbing. I realized that most people don't understand how their investments work. And what's worse is that it's probable that your financial advisor, human resources manager and CPA don't understand how they work either. I know that is a horrible thing to say but if it's not true, that means they do understand how they work and they are sabotaging your retirement plan. Read on …

What if you could do better than what the local bank is paying on your certificate of deposit? What if you didn't have to worry about the ups and downs of the stock market? What if you could retire at the age YOU decide — even if it is before age 59½ — and not be penalized? What if your retirement income was not subject to income tax? What if your Social Security benefits were not penalized? What if your Medicare premiums were not increased because of your successful planning? I know, I know. It all sounds too good to be true. BUT if all of this were true, would you have the confidence you need to get your retirement savings plan back on track?

The answer to many of the retirement planning challenges we face today lies in a concept dating back to June 18, 1536. Through the years, the concept has been improved upon, but for the most part, it has always been shunned as a retirement planning tool. Why? It's nontraditional and goes against prevailing financial planning thinking. Yet during the period of 2000–2010, which is commonly referred to as "The Lost Decade," this concept outperformed the S&P 500 by 102.69%. No, that's not a typo. It is misunderstood and misrepresented but has the power to increase your retirement income by thousands, maybe even tens of thousands.

So why aren't financial planners touting this concept? I mean there are hundreds, no doubt thousands of people who are smarter than me. The information I am about to share with you is not rocket science although I do have a bachelor of science degree in physics. I over-analyze everything. What can I say? I love numbers!

The fact is, I'm really not that much different than most people. My retirement account is not fully funded, my taxes have increased and I am making adjustments to my discretionary spending just like most people. The main difference is I have had enough, and I'm not afraid to upturn conventional thinking. Most of the things you are about to read will probably make you mad — mad at your accountant, mad at your financial advisor, mad at your favorite financial guru because they haven't talked to you about this. Well, I'm not sorry for what I am about to share. Actually, shame on them for not telling you first!

PART 1
SOME INCONVENIENT TRUTHS

Chapter 1 | Suze Orman-ism

As a veteran of the financial services industry, I have followed financial advisor and author Suze Orman for years. She grew up on the south side of Chicago and says she was never very good in school. In 1973, she left the University of Illinois one class short of graduating and drove to California, where she became a waitress. After about six years, Orman decided she wanted to open her own restaurant. She shared the idea with one of her regular customers, and before her shift was over that day, she had checks and commitments in hand for $50,000. Orman's charm, personality and strength of character inspired devotion from others very early on.

Acknowledging she knew very little about investing, Orman engaged the help of a financial advisor who ultimately lost her $50,000 for the restaurant. Determined to move forward, she learned everything she could about investing and became a broker for Merrill Lynch shortly thereafter. In 1983, she left Merrill Lynch to join Prudential Bache Securities. While at Prudential, she earned her Certified Financial Planner designation, and in 1987, Orman left to start her own firm, the Suze Orman Financial Group.

In 1995, Orman released her first book. Her second book landed on the best-sellers list in 1997, and in 1999, Orman was named one of Smart Money magazine's "Power Brokers," defined as those who have most influenced the mutual-fund industry. Orman has been called a "force in the world of personal finance" and a "one-woman financial-advice powerhouse" by USA Today. She also was profiled in Worth magazine's 100th issue (October 2001) as among those "who have revolutionized the way America thinks about money."

More popular titles followed, and in 2003, she received accolades for her television series, "The Suze Orman Show." A sought-after speaker, Orman has lectured widely throughout the United States, Asia and South America, helping people change the way they think about money.

With success comes responsibility. Orman's CFP designation holds her to the highest principles and standards in the industry. This accomplishment afforded Orman the credentials she needed to gain the respect of millions of investors, young and old. Though she has been labeled a "Power Broker" and a "one-woman financial-advice powerhouse," she makes it clear in an article for the The Daily Beast in November 2013 that her interest is personal finance. In the article she is quoted as saying, "Remember, my topic is personal finance. It's not what stock should you buy, where's the economy, it's not a deep dive like that. There's plenty of people that will tell you about stocks and money." Wait a second. Is she saying she is not a financial advisor?

I thought I was going crazy. But apparently, I'm not the only one who is a bit confused. In an article published by Forbes earlier this year, Carmine Gallo gets it wrong, too. He writes, "More than 300,000 financial advisors in the United States provide saving, investing and retirement advice, but only one made the top 10 of the Forbes 2013 list of the most influential celebrities: Suze Orman."

My curiosity got the best of me so I did a little research and it's absolutely true. As of the writing of this book, the last time Orman was reportedly with a FINRA firm was in 1991. Now it makes sense. When her second book hit the best-sellers list? She told People Magazine, "It was at that point that I made the change from being a financial advisor who wanted simply to give a book to my clients to a No. 1 New York Times best-selling author."

Gallo goes on to talk about Orman's passion to help people avoid crushing financial debt and the energy that fills the room when she speaks. When you combine passion and energy, you get likability. Although she maintains her CFP designation, Orman has transformed herself into an influential celebrity. And an influential celebrity she is! This influence carries with it a tremendous amount of responsibility where I come from. Her following is ginormous. If she says drink purple Kool-Aid for 30 days in a row at precisely 3:57 a.m., a lot of people might do it! I'm exaggerating, but you get the point. You may think that is funny, but when it comes to your money and what to do with it, funny is not the word that comes to my mind.

Orman may say that's not her topic but her books, website and television show say differently. The themes are strong and repetitive. Sometimes it's not what she says that concerns me as much as what she doesn't say. So what? Why does any of this even matter? Because millions of people hang on her every word and many of them are the ones whose money will run out before they reach their mid-70s.

In chapter 18 of Orman's third book, "The Courage to Be Rich," we read:

"What do we think, say and do with our money? Too often, we base our thoughts, phrase our words, and take action based on myths that have been passed down from parent to child, financial advisor to client, real-estate agent to homebuyer, car salesman or insurance agent to consumer; from colleague to colleague, neighbor to neighbor, or friend to friend. The problem is that when financial reality hits — perhaps in our 40s, 50s, or even later — these financial myths explode, making us wish that we had been paying close attention to our own financial reality all along."

Oh, my goodness. Of all the advice Orman has given over the years, this truly is paramount. Ironically, it seems Orman herself has fallen victim to financial myths; myths that she continues to pass along to innocent victims who read her books, watch her shows and listen to her CDs. I have dedicated countless hours to revealing these myths in the chapters that follow. You will not be disappointed by what you discover. You hold in your hands information that has the power to change the face of retirement for this country. If I didn't have your attention before, I trust I do now.

Chapter 2 |
Some People Are Flat Out Wrong, And It's Not Always Their Fault

The 2014 Retirement Confidence Survey reports that 34% of workers and 31% of retirees surveyed stated their No. 1 reason for not following the advice of a financial advisor was they did not trust the advice they were given. That is astounding!

This says a lot about our financial services industry. Now that I know what I know, I can understand that.

In 1996, I spent three weeks in Connecticut training with Sandy Weill and Jamie Dimon to be a financial consultant for Citigroup's Smith Barney (later sold to Morgan Stanley). I mean that should count for something, right? Dimon is the chairman, president and CEO of JP Morgan Chase, and Weill was the CEO of Citigroup until October 2003. Looking back, I realize I was not trained to be a financial consultant. Oh yes, that was the title they gave me and I coveted it, but I did not receive the proper training to become a financial anything. I was however trained to be a fantastic salesman of the company's products. It wasn't until I challenged the "traditional" way of thinking and began to think for myself that I discovered how to successfully coach my clients into retirement.

A few years ago, I was sitting in my office with a couple completing their annual review. I explained that the previous 12-month return for their mutual fund was 10%. I felt the pride swell up inside me as I pulled out the glossy fact sheet that the company had provided so they could see the performance for themselves. The year before, we had invested $100,000 into this fund. The clients looked at their statement, then looked back at me. With a little bit of hesitation, Joe asked, "Why do we only have a little over $107,000? Shouldn't we have closer to $110,000?" This was a great question and I thanked him for asking it.

I reminded Joe and his wife, Sheila, that they had purchased the "A" shares of this particular fund. Joe immediately perked up and said, "That's right! I remember. Instead of paying the normal rate of 5.75%, we qualified for a discount."

Joe and Sheila were saving for retirement. I had recommended a growth fund that had averaged double-digit returns since its inception in 1973. This particular fund had three main share classes: A, B and C shares. Basically, you get to pick how you want to pay your commission. Remember, no one works for free. When I teach this subject in my investment class, I draw a chart on the board something like the one you see below:

	A-share	B-shares	C-shares
Maximum charge	5.75%	0	0
Internal fee	0.70	1.46	1.50
CDSC 0	0	5/4/4/3/2/1/0	1/0

Each share class includes a maximum sales charge, an internal fee and a CDSC, better known as a contingent deferred sales charge. As we examine the chart, keep the following in mind: A-shares are like paying cash for a new car. B-shares are like financing your new car (you will always pay more for a car you finance). C-shares are like leasing a car. I don't know about you, but I'm not a fan of leasing. I believe it is the most expensive way to get a car.

C-shares

Now, I would expect you to initially select C-shares. On the surface it does look like a pretty good deal (so does leasing until you learn about all the extra fees). You pay nothing up front, 1.5% annually and it costs you nothing to leave the fund after year one. The determining factor here is how long you expect to own the fund. Joe and Sheila are 20 years away from retirement. If they were to purchase C-shares, they would pay 1.5% every year for 10 years before converting to F-1 shares and paying a reduced fee of 0.71 annually. That's 15% in fees before converting! Not looking so good now, huh?

B-shares

The next obvious choice then is B-shares. Again, you pay nothing up front, 1.46% annually and if you liquidate your fund anytime during the first six years, you will pay a deferred sales charge not to exceed 5%. You're thinking this could work. Joe and Sheila are 20 years from retirement, so there is no chance they would have to pay that 5% contingent deferred sales charge. Most B-shares automatically convert to A-shares after eight years. So the internal fee would drop from 1.46 to 0.70 in the eighth year. Some quick math tells us that after eight years, they will have paid 11.68% in fees before converting. Hey! We're moving in the right direction.

A-shares

No one really wants to talk about A-shares. We love the fact there is no contingent deferred sales charge, but no one wants 5.75% shaved off the top on day one. I get that, but things aren't always what they seem. After eight years, how much would Joe and Sheila have paid in total fees and commissions? 5.75% plus 5.6% (0.7 x 8 years) equals 11.35%. Okay. It's a little less than B-shares overall for the first eight years, but you still can't bring yourself to pay that 5.75% commission. Trust me. I get it. But wait! There's more! (Don't you just love those infomercials!)

When Joe and Sheila came to me for advice, they already owned some mutual funds. As we considered how to invest Joe's rollover from his previous company, I explained to them how they could reduce their commission by utilizing their Rights of Accumulation. Under this provision, a mutual fund company will allow you to add all of your A-share positions together in order to reach a break point and receive a discount on any new A-share purchase. Let's say you have $25,000 in a joint account and $25,000 in an IRA. As far as the mutual fund company is concerned, you have $50,000 invested with them and would qualify for a discount based upon the following schedule:

Investment	Offering Price
Less than 25,000	5.75%
$25,000 but less than $50,000	5.00
$50,000 but less than $100,000	4.50
$100,000 but less than $250,000	3.50
$250,000 but less than $500,000	2.50
$500,000 but less than $750,000	2.00
$750,000 but less than $1 million	1.50
$1 million or more	none

So, if you were going to invest an additional $25,000 instead of paying 5.75% commission, you would pay only 4.5%. Hmmm. A-shares are starting to get a bit more interesting. But wait. There's more! Joe and Sheila also had mentioned that one of their IRA certificates of deposit would be maturing in 10 months. They had been happy with the past performance of their mutual funds and planned to add the proceeds of the CD when it matured. That would be an additional $25,000. I began to explain yet another provision to Joe and Sheila called an LOI or Letter of Intent. Although this is not a physical "letter," it allows an investor to receive a discount on today's purchase based upon a commitment to make an additional purchase within the next 13 months. How cool is that? Now instead of paying 5.75% commission, they would only have to pay 3.5% commission. That brings their total for commissions and fees down to 9.1% for the first eight years, a savings of 2.58% over the B-shares. Note that if you utilize the Letter of Intent provision and do not keep your end of the deal, the mutual fund company will come back after the 13th month and charge the additional commission that you would have otherwise paid.

There's one more factor you should keep in mind when determining which share class best meets your needs. Commissions are charged on your initial investment one time and you're done. Internal fees are assessed on your account value. So, what exactly does that mean? It means if you elect to purchase $100,000 of A-shares, you would pay $3,500 one time. Your internal fee of 0.70 would be based upon your account value each year AND you could liquidate your shares at any time without incurring an additional fee.

With B-shares, you don't have an upfront fee but your internal fees are higher and you have to pay a fee to leave within the first six years. Let's look at an example:

Account value	A-shares (3.5+.70)	B-shares (0+1.46)
$100,000	$3,500	$0
$110,000	$770	$1,606
$115,000	$805	$1,679
$125,000	$875	$1,825
Fee to liquidate, year 4	$0	$3,750
Total costs	*$5,950*	*$8,860*

In this example, we invested $100,000. The account grew from one year to the next and in year four, the position was liquidated. As you can see, even though $3,500 was shaved off the top on day one, A-shares proved to be much less expensive than B-shares.

As I said earlier, things aren't always what they seem. There are a million different scenarios we could have used here. Sometimes A-shares will cost less and sometimes B-shares will cost less. The point of me sharing this information with you is to arm you with the information you need in order to make the best decision for your family if you should decide that you absolutely cannot live without mutual funds.

Note that no-Load funds are not free. You cannot simply pick a fund because it charges the lowest fee. Remember, you get what you pay for. When comparing mutual funds, you also should look at the overall performance of the fund. Would you be willing to pay a commission or a higher fee if the fund produced a higher return?

As I finished Joe and Sheila's review that afternoon, I was proud of my work. I had recommended a fund with a historical double-digit average return and utilized the Rights of Accumulation and Letter of Intent provisions to get them in at the best possible price. I had done a good job.

Time flew by and before I knew it, Joe and Sheila were scheduled to come in for another review. In preparation for our meeting, I pulled up the performance numbers for the fund they owned and began to compare them to the actual account value. It had been a volatile couple of years, but the fund had managed to average 8%. With an additional 8%, Joe and Sheila should have been sitting on about $115,500. But they weren't. I double-checked my math. $107,000 times 8% equals $115,560. Why did they only have $114,000? I reviewed the account, confirming there had been no withdrawals. I thought perhaps I had misread the fund fact sheet. Maybe the 8% was "before" they deducted the internal fees. Nope. I confirmed that FINRA requires all performance numbers to be reported net of all fees. So what in the world was going on?

I pulled out a pencil and started to calculate the performance by hand. What I discovered rocked me to my very core. This couldn't be happening. I had been in the financial services industry for more than 20 years. I was licensed. I had been professionally trained!

Consider this five-year segment of market performance.

Year 1	+10%
Year 2	-32%
Year 3	+40%
Year 4	+12%
Year 5	+10%

If you total the numbers (10-32+40+12+10=40) and divide by 5, you arrive at an 8% average return for that five-year segment. Now apply this same market performance to an actual $1,000 investment.

Year 1	$1,000	+ $100 (10%)	= $1,100
Year 2	$1,100	- $352 (-32%)	= $748
Year 3	$748	+ $299.20 (+40%)	= $1,047.20
Year 4	$1,047.20	+ $125.66 (+12%)	= $1,172.86
Year 5	$1,172.86	+ $117.29 (+10%)	= $1,290.15

The gain of $290.15 as a percentage of the original investment ($1,000) is 29.01%. Divide 29.01 by 5 years and you arrive at an average return of 5.80%.

The market had averaged 8% but the investor had only received 5.8%. How could this happen? All the marketing materials reported an 8% average return for the last five years. The fund fact sheets had been approved by FINRA. How could they be wrong? Technically, they were right. The average for that five-year segment was 8%.

Think about this. If the market dropped 50% today and then gained 50% tomorrow, I imagine the Wall Street headlines would read something like this on the third day:"Shew! We dodged a bullet; market flat." Do the math. -50+50 = 0/2 days is an average of 0% for those two days. So they can market a 0% return or flat market. Now, imagine you had $100 invested in this so-called "flat" market. After day one, your $100 would be worth $50. On day two, your $50 would gain 50% or $25 bringing your account back to even. Right? Well, that would be really nice, but you, my friend, now have $75 leaving your account DOWN 25% in what many financial advisors would call a "flat" market.

I felt weak and thought I was going to throw up. I had participated in countless meetings over the years; completed continuing education requirements to maintain my licenses; and not once had anyone explained how the stock market truly works. All I could think about were my clients. I had worked so hard to help them. I was devastated.

Market returns are NOT investor returns! They aren't even close.

Chapter 3 | Retirement Planning Gone Bad

For years I had been helping people plan for retirement. I had prepared countless financial plans and was always careful to use conservative assumptions in my projections. I would tell my clients, "I'd rather have an upside surprise than a downside disappointment." Well, I'm here to tell ya, this discovery left me both surprised and disappointed at the same time!

So, were all the plans I took so much pride in creating wrong? And if mine were wrong, did that mean all the other financial advisors plans were wrong, too? Surely not! I started to feel sick to my stomach again. No wonder the baby boomers don't have enough money to retire! I remember audibly telling myself, "just … calm … down." I thought, "Maybe I am just overreacting." I mean, come on! That would just be crazy, right?

All financial advisors/consultants/planners use some form of software that utilizes a future value calculator. A future value calculator tells us how much your money will be worth at some point in the future. We enter the investment amount, the rate of return we expect you to receive, how often it will compound and your retirement date. We push a button and poof, we instantly know how much money you should have to live on when you reach retirement. Sound familiar?

My curiosity got the best of me. I went to www.timevalue.com and pulled up their future-value calculator. I entered today's date, a date five years in the future, $1,000 as my investment and 8% as my rate of return compounding annually. I pushed the button and $1,469.33 appeared. For the sake of my own sanity, I had to do the math.

I grabbed a pencil, and wrote down the following figures:

Year 1	$1,000	$80 (8%)	= $1,080.00
Year 2	$1,080	$86.40 (8%)	= $1,166.40
Year 3	$1,166.40	$93.31 (8%)	= $1,259.71
Year 4	$1,259.71	$100.78 (8%)	= $1,360.49
Year 5	$1,360.49	$108.84 (8%)	= $1,469.33

I stared at these numbers for a minute and then I remembered the numbers I had calculated for Joe and Sheila's account review.

Year 1	$1,000	+ $100 (10%)	= $1,100.00
Year 2	$1,100	- $352 (-32%)	= $748.00
Year 3	$748	+ $299.20 (+40%)	= $1,047.20
Year 4	$1,047.20	+ $125.66 (+12%)	= $1,172.86
Year 5	$1,172.86	+ $117.29 (+10%)	= $1,290.15

Remember, the average return for Joe and Sheila's five-year segment is also 8% (10-32+40+12+10 =40/5=8). You could have knocked me over with a feather! The future-value calculator estimated I would have $1,469.33 after five years when in reality I only had $1,290.15. I am short $179.18. That may not seem like a big deal to you so let's put it into perspective.

A $1,000 investment would be short $179.18
A 10,000 investment would be short $1,791.80
A 100,000 investment would be short $17,918.00
A 1,000,000 investment would be short $179,180.

Are you starting to get the picture? The account is short 17.92%! But why? It took me a minute, but I finally saw it. Yep, there it was. How had I missed it? More importantly, how had all of us missed it? I now refer to it as "the hole." In year two, financially we stepped in a pile of … oops, I mean we stepped in a hole — and a big one at that, down 32%. Not only did we lose our 10% gain from the previous year, we lost more than 25% of our principal, too. Our ending balances after year two was $748. Seems we lost more like 35%, doesn't it (10 + 25)? Yea, you're starting to see how dangerous it is to use averages to project future values.

But hey, year three was great! We recovered from the 32% loss in year two and are 8% to the good, right? Not so fast. Climbing out of a hole is never easy, and when you're in over your head, it's much harder. Here's the deal. When the market goes back up 40% in year three, you only have $748 to earn 40% on. Can you imagine how great it would be if you still had the $1,100 from year 1 to earn 40% on? Holy cow! Now that would be something to get excited about!

If you or anyone you know has ever had a financial plan prepared by a member of the financial services industry, I'm afraid it may not be worth the paper it is written on. The biggest challenge financial advisors face is trying to accurately predict something that goes up AND down. Do you realize that if the market never had a down day, I would not be writing this? Even if we only earned 2 or 3%, every year we would always be adding to last year's ending balance (a lot like those future value calculators). The problem is the market does not go straight up. Even in a year where the overall return is positive, there will be down days and you will lose money; money that you may or may not get back.

Financial myth #1: You can accurately project the future value of a variable product using an average rate of return. I think we've proved beyond a shadow of a doubt that you clearly cannot accurately project the future value of a variable product using an average rate of return. BUSTED! (I just love watching Jamie and Adam blow things up on MythBusters.)

I still couldn't believe it. After all these years, why had no one shared this information with me? I felt like the industry had let me down. It's worth noting here that when you access the future-value calculator at www.futurevalues.com, you will see a link at the bottom of the page for a "calculator disclaimer." Click on it and you will see the following:

"The information provided by these calculators is intended for illustrative purposes only and is not intended to purport actual user-defined parameters. The default figures shown are hypothetical and may not be applicable to your individual situation. Be sure to consult a financial professional prior to relying on the results."

Chapter 4 | From Bad to Worse

Why do we put off until tomorrow what we can do today?

Because of my recent discovery of how the market truly works and that I cannot accurately project the future value of a variable product using an average rate of return, I began to question everything. If I were going to do the best job possible for my clients and right this wrong that I felt personally responsible for, I had to find out if there was anything else I didn't know.

Any financial advisor or Certified Financial Planner will tell you the first thing you must have is an emergency fund. We may differ on exactly how much you need to have in this account. But we will all agree a "rainy-day fund" should be your first priority. Next, we look at your debt to determine if any or all of the money you are considering for an investment today should be used to lower your credit card and/or loan balances. Once your rainy-day fund and debt are in check, we get laser-focused on reducing your income taxes. After all, if we can reduce your taxes, you get to keep more of what you make, right?

The very first thing we want to know is whether or not your employer offers a 401(k) plan. If they do, our next question will be, "Do they offer a match?" As far back as I can remember, I have been trained to tell my clients to max out their 401(k) contributions. Why? When you make contributions to the plan, a couple of things happen. First, if you make $100,000 this year and contribute $10,000 to your 401(k) plan, the IRS will only charge you income tax on the difference ($90,000). That's a $2,500 savings this year for married couples and a $2,800 savings for individual filers (see 2014 Federal Income Tax Brackets). Second, the earnings on your contributions grow tax-deferred. Basically, you pay no income tax on your contributions or earnings until they are withdrawn. Now if your plan offers a match that is even better! Who doesn't want free money? Granted, many company matches have been reduced or suspended, but there still are plans out there that will match your contribution up to a limit. So, if you are one of the lucky ones whose company offers a 401(k) plan AND a matching contribution, you should go for it! Right?

The Fourth Law of Financial Freedom from Suze Orman's book, "The 9 Steps to Financial Freedom" is "It's Not What You Make — It's What You Get To Keep." She says, "Money that goes into a retirement fund is money you do not have to pay taxes on until you take it out … . Depending on your income tax bracket, you might be able to keep up to 35 percent more of your money (the highest federal tax bracket through 2012). Because of the tax savings, contributing the maximum to your retirement account right now will not deprive you of as much current income as you might fear. And where it will make a vast difference is in what you'll have to spend later."

Orman then challenges you to complete an exercise. She says, "If you are covered at work by a 401(k), 403(b), or SIMPLE plan, I want you to go into your human resources office and up your contribution. You must contribute at least enough to qualify for the maximum matching employer contribution. That match is a free bonus you do not want to pass up. After you have achieved that, your focus should be on also funding a Roth IRA. Then, if you have the ability to save even more, you can increase your work-based contributions even higher. The absolute best move is if you can fully fund your work retirement plan as well as a Roth IRA."

I absolutely love this law — It's not what you make — it's what you get to keep. Who wants to pay taxes anyway? Not me! Suze's advice here is no different than what me and every other financial advisor have been trained to recommend. As a matter of fact, one of the first jobs I ever had offered a 401(k) plan and they encouraged me to participate. I remember asking the manager why he thought it was such a good idea to put money into a 401(k) plan. He explained that I wouldn't have to pay income tax on the money I put into the plan and that the company would add 50 cents for every dollar I contributed up to 3% of my salary. He called it "free money." I was young but I wasn't stupid. I knew there would come a day when I would have to pay up. He confirmed that I would in fact have to pay taxes on all the money (my contributions, the "free money" and any earnings) when I withdrew it at retirement, adding that when I retired I would more than likely be in a lower income tax bracket because I would make less money in retirement than when I was working. Made sense to me!

I like the way Orman says it in her book, "The Road To Wealth." In chapter 6, she writes, "for every dollar you put into your 401(k) plan, your employer might give you 50 cents, up to a certain percentage of what you put in. Some generous employers will match any percentage of your contributions dollar for dollar. If your employer does match any percentage of your 401(k) contributions, you cannot afford to pass this up — this is free money. Think about it — if your employer matches 50 cents on the dollar, for every dollar it matches you are essentially getting an automatic 50 percent return on that money." Holy cow! That is one heck of a return. I think it is safe to say Orman is a fan of 401(k) plans.

In my endeavor to now question everything I ever knew about finances and investing, I began to think more about tax deferral and what it truly means. The term itself is pretty self-explanatory: to delay tax. Why would we want to delay our taxes? To save money! I know, I know. We've already been over this but I need you to stay with me here. I'm pretty sure we have been hoodwinked again.

When you contribute $10,000 to your 401(k), what are you hoping will happen? You are hoping it will grow, get bigger. As I sat there thinking about the money growing from one year to the next, I couldn't help but think about a small little apple seed that over time with proper care will flourish and grow into an apple tree, perhaps a very large apple tree. As I took a deep breath, I closed my eyes and started to shake my head. They had gotten me again! I suddenly realized that if the money got bigger, so would the tax liability. Think about it. If you put $10,000 into your 401(k) and it turns into $15,000, you now owe tax on $15,000 not $10,000. That's a 50% increase in account value and a 50% increase in taxes. Assume you are currently in the 15% tax bracket and that you will remain in the 15% tax bracket when you retire:

$$\$10,000 \times 0.15 = \$1,500$$
$$\$15,000 \times 0.15 = \$2,250$$
$$\$2,250 - \$1,500 = \$750$$

Pay $1,500 now, or pay $2,250 later.

Now, if you think you are going to drop into the 10% tax bracket during retirement, you need to think again. In order to fall into the 10% tax bracket (currently the lowest tax bracket for 2014), married couples can have no more than $18,150 of taxable income and individuals are limited to $9,075. I don't know about you, but I sure plan to receive more than $9,075 per year when I retire.

Fact: If your 401(k) grows, you will owe more, not less, in taxes when you retire.

Financial myth #2: Tax deferral saves money. BUSTED!

As I sat in my office letting this all sink in, I couldn't help but think about our current economic conditions. Our country's outstanding debt currently sits at $17,781,487,901,300.17 (www. brillig.com/debt_clock). Do you think taxes are going to go up, down or stay the same between now and when you retire? I really don't see how they can go down. The Center on Budget and Policy Priorities reported on April 11, 2013, that federal income taxes on middle-income families remain near historic lows. The debt has to be paid. Taxes have to go up. I know you don't want to hear that, but ignoring it is not going to make it go away. The question is, where will income tax rates be when you retire? There is absolutely no way to know the answer to that question.

You should know that if you ask any CPA, financial advisor, certified financial planner or human resource manager whether or not they think it is a good idea to contribute to a 401(k) plan, they will all say "yes." Now that I know the truth about tax deferral, why would I ever want to put myself in such a vulnerable situation?

How do you stop a runaway train going 110 mph? And if you can't stop it, do you have time to get out of its path?

| Basics of Financial Planning

I thought back to the early days of my career ... all the way back to the basics of financial planning, where it all begins. When I meet with a potential client for the first time, I am on a fact-finding mission. I use this opportunity to get to know them better in order to determine if I can help them or not. I ask questions about their income and expenses, their assets and liabilities, their families, changes in future expenses, retirement plans and whether or not they are charitably inclined. I know that sounds like I am terribly nosey, but I have to know. When it comes right down to it, I am a financial doctor.

Imagine for a moment you are sitting in the emergency room. Your left arm is aching and it is difficult for you to breathe. The doctor comes in and asks, "what's the problem?" and you say "I'm not really sure," to which he replies, "Are you having any pain?" You say, "You know, doc, that's kinda personal." How in the world can you expect the doctor to properly diagnose your condition and prescribe the best medication to get you back on your feet if you refuse to answer his questions?

Let's take this a step further. Because you have withheld the fact that your left arm is aching and it is difficult for you to breathe, the doctor says, "Take an aspirin and call me in the morning." Provided you live through the night, tomorrow when you wake up you might say something like, "I don't feel any better ... in fact, I feel worse. Doctor so-in-so is an idiot! That aspirin didn't help me at all." I think you get my point. Albeit difficult, you must stand before your financial advisor financially naked if you expect the recommendations to produce positive results.

Chapter 5 | Stop the Madness!

With the tax-deferral myth busted, I had to take a really hard look at 401(k) plans. I mean, if there is no tax benefit to delaying taxes, then how is this plan helping you? Well, there is the company match. After all, that is "free money." Hmmm. My Dad told me more than once, "Nothing in life is free." I decided I needed to learn everything there was to know about this "free money."

For starters, I learned that even though your company may offer a 401(k) plan, you may or may not be eligible to participate. According to the 2014 Retirement Confidence Survey, "One of the primary vehicles workers use to save for retirement is an employer-sponsored retirement savings plan, such as a 401(k). Eighty-two percent of eligible workers (38% of all workers) say they participate in such a plan with their current employer, and another 8% of eligible workers report they have money in such a plan, although they are not currently contributing."

Did you catch that? Eighty-two percent of eligible workers (38% of all workers) say they participate in a plan with their current employer. So just because you work for an employer who offers a 401(k) plan does not mean you can contribute to it. If a 401(k) plan is considered to be one of the primary vehicles used to save for retirement, why are you not allowed to use it?

Employees must meet certain eligibility requirements to participate in the plan their employer adopts.

He or she has reached age 21

An employee can be excluded for not having reached a minimum age (which cannot exceed age 21) but cannot be excluded for having reached a maximum age. For instance, an employee cannot be excluded from the plan because he or she is, say, 100 years old.

He or she has at least one year of service

This requirement is two years if the plan is not a 401(k) plan and provides that after not more than two years of service the employee has a non-forfeitable right to all his or her accrued benefit (i.e. all contributions are 100% vested). For qualified plan purposes, a year of service is generally 1,000 hours of service performed during the plan year. Employees who do not perform 1,000 hours of service are not considered to have performed one year of service, even if services were performed for a 12-month period.

Imagine you have just become eligible to participate in your company 401(k) plan only to learn that your job has been eliminated because of downsizing. Now what? You have to find a new job and re-qualify (provided the new employer offers a 401(k) plan), which forces you to wait up to two more years before becoming eligible to contribute to what is one of the primary vehicles used today to save for retirement.

Forgive me, but I must point out that matters could be worse. Did you notice the little word "vested" in the description of the eligibility requirements above? Vesting refers to your portion of ownership in the money that has been given to you" ... the "free money."

By law and by definition, you are always 100% vested in any money you contribute to your 401(k). This means if you change jobs, all the money you contributed from your paycheck is yours.

To encourage loyalty, employers can make their contributions (the "free money") subject to vesting schedules, which means they can dangle their contributions in front of you like a carrot — the more years you work, the more of their contributions you get to keep.

Vesting schedules come in three basic types:

• Immediate vesting: Just as the name implies, employees with this type of vesting plan gain 100% ownership of their employer's matching money as soon as it lands in their accounts.

• Cliff vesting: Cliff vesting plans transfer 100% ownership to the employee in one big chunk after a specific period of service. Workers have no right to any of their matching contributions if they leave before that period expires. But the day they reach the landmark date, they own it all. Federal law puts a three-year limit on cliff vesting schedules in qualified retirement plans, such as a 401(k) or a 403(b).

• Graded vesting: Graded vesting gives employees gradually increasing ownership of matching contributions as their length of service increases, resulting in 100% ownership.

This presents a problem. The days when people held one job for all, or most, of their working life are gone. Today, the average person changes jobs 10-15 to (with an average of 11 job changes) during his or her career. So if you are counting on your employer match to help you reach your retirement goal, you may want to think again.

Free money? You may never even see this money! And if YOU don't get to keep the money when you change jobs, who does? I found out that most plans use the forfeited contributions to pay the plan expenses. Basically, it goes back to the company! So to encourage our loyalty, companies dangle this "free money" carrot in front of us. Once they lure us into a plan that we now know costs more in taxes, not less, they snatch it back! That's just wrong.

In Orman's book, "The Money Class," she says, "More than 20% of workers don't contribute enough to earn the maximum their company offers to match. I don't care what other financial issues you are dealing with in your life — you must always take advantage of a match when it is offered. That match is just like a bonus, and if you turn your back on this bonus it is literally throwing money away." Seems to me the only money we are throwing away is our own!

So why is Orman and most other financial advisors screaming at the top of our lungs to contribute the maximum to your 401(k)? The industry has trained us to believe this is a good option.

I began to wonder if there was something in it for employers? Turns out, there is. One of the tax advantages of sponsoring a 401(k) plan is employer contributions are deductible on the employer's federal income tax return. Okay, so companies get a little help on their tax bill. That doesn't seem like a big enough reason to send us down this dead-end road. There is an entire industry built around the 401(k) plan. I wanted to know who was really benefitting from these plans.

Until recently, it has been nearly impossible for a 401(k) participant to know exactly how much he or she is paying in fees. In 2012, the Department of Labor changed all of that, forcing companies to disclose the costs of 401(k) retirement plans. An article published by Forbes on March 11, 2013, titled "401(k) Plans Are Still Widely Misunderstood" (I couldn't agree more!), Ashlea Ebeling writes, "Looking at the total plan expenses, including administrative and record-keeping ... the average total expenses for a small plan in 2012 was 1.46%, with a range between a low of 0.38% and a high of 1.97%. Investment fees continued their downward trend. Small plan average investment expenses declined from 1.38% in 2011 to 1.37% in 2012, and large plan average investment expenses declined from 1.05% to 1.00%." That's a mouthful, I know. So let me help you out. In 2012, 401(k) fees for a small plan were as high as 3.34% and they were HIGHER in 2011. I hate to point this out, but that fee is charged EVERY YEAR. Good Lord!

Administrative fees, record-keeping fees and investment expenses totaling 3.34%? It is no wonder the average 401(k) account balance is only $89,300 as of year-end 2013 (and that's a new high)! Do you realize the impact 3.34% has on your 401(k) balance every year? Think about this. If the funds in your plan appreciated 2% this year, your account would DROP by 1.34%! Yes. In a year where your funds delivered a positive return, your account balance would be less than it was the year before unless you contribute on a regular basis. So most people don't even see the money leaking out of their account.

Financial Myth #3 – The 401(k) match is free money. BUSTED!

Sounds to me like the only people getting "free money" is the IRS, the plan administrators and the mutual fund companies.

As of March 31, 2014, 401(k) plans held an estimated $4.3 trillion in assets. The IRS is licking their chops as that number continues to build. Do you understand it is in complete control of how much income tax you will pay on your tax-deferred 401(k)? How is that, you ask? Because anytime the government thinks it needs more money, it increases our income tax rates. Don't think for one minute, they don't have their eye on the GIANT IOU better known as the 401(k) industry!

I don't know about you, but I've had enough of these 401(k) plans. Even though plan sponsors are scrambling to reduce fees because of the new disclosure requirements, I see very little, if any, good that can come out of them. I'm out, as they say on the TV show "Shark Tank."

Chapter 6 | The Fine Print

Have you ever been surfing the Internet and stumbled across a product you think you just can't live without? Or maybe you're a victim of a late-night infomercial. We are so excited about losing 30 pounds in two weeks or going from bald to a full head of hair in less than 30 days that we cannot get our credit cards out fast enough (yes, I'm a victim, too). We give them all the information they ask for, accept every free offer that flashes on the screen, and then anxiously wait by our mailbox the next day. What? You didn't upgrade to overnight shipping? Before long we discover it wasn't everything it was cracked up to be. As we read the fine print, we suddenly realize we have authorized them to charge our credit card monthly for the next 12 months! We send emails and make nasty phone calls, but nothing works. The only thing we can do is suck it up and pay for the junk!

With a commitment to never participate in or recommend anyone else participate in a 401(k) plan ever again, I went on a mission to figure out exactly what my clients need to do in order to cancel this "financial subscription" without losing the shirt on their back.

The easy part is to march right into your human resource department tomorrow morning and sign whatever paperwork necessary to STOP all future contributions to your 401(k) plan. I call this part "stop the bleeding." I know that sounds extreme and goes against everything you have ever heard before but the fact is, your retirement savings account is hemorrhaging and in need of immediate attention. Let's review. The volatility of the stock market could leave your retirement plan short 17.92% or more; tax-deferral does not save money; it costs money; the company match is a hoax; and your plan expenses could be as high as 3.34% EVERY SINGLE YEAR.

Folks, you cannot AFFORD to contribute to a 401(k) plan. It's that simple!

By the way, if you have been suckered into contributing to a 403(b) plan (a 401(k) plan for nonprofits), a 457 plan (deferred compensation plan offered mainly to government employees), a SEP plan (simplified employee pension), a SIMPLE IRA (savings incentive match plan for employees) or an IRA (Individual Retirement Account) for the most part, they operate the same way!

Now for the hard part, how do we salvage what you already have in the plan? That's a great question and it can be done, but it won't be easy. It's fine if you don't want to put any more of your money into the plan, but taking your money out, well that's another story all together. We need to review the distribution rules: the IRS rules and the plan rules.

You remember enough from those 401(k) enrollment meetings to know that if you take a distribution before age 59½, you will owe a 10% penalty on top of whatever income tax may be due. But you don't care. Tomorrow when you march into the human resource department to sign whatever forms are necessary to stop contributing to your 401(k), you also are going to sign whatever forms are necessary to liquidate the entire account, pay the 10% penalty and be done with this madness! Not so fast, cowboy.

The IRS may allow you to liquidate your plan and pay the 10% penalty (boy, wouldn't they love to have that extra money), but your plan doesn't. I know you are REALLY upset with me right now, but you need to know these rules. I always say, " If I know the rules, I can play the game." Per your plan document, you are eligible to liquidate your account when and only when you meet certain requirements. If you are still working, you can access funds from an old 401(k) plan once you reach 59½, BUT you may NOT have the same access to funds inside the 401(k) plan at the company where you currently work.

I know. You want to beat your head against the wall, right? "How can they do that? It's my money, and the IRS says I can have it? Why won't the company let me have my money?" you ask. Buried deep in the stack of papers signed was this little provision that said you only have access to your money if you separate from service (quit, get fired, are downsized, retire or die). Remember, they were getting as much as 3.34% in annual fees in 2012. They don't want to lose that revenue stream any sooner than they have to.

What if you were to change jobs? When you are younger than 55 and separate from service, you really have three options: request your account balance be rolled over to an IRA; request a check for the account balance; or any combination of the previous two options. The entire account balance less any matching contribution that has not yet vested is eligible to be rolled over to an IRA to continue your journey down Tax-Deferral Lane. Did I mention that street is a dead-end?

In my professional opinion, rolling over to an IRA is not going to solve our problem, but it can help solve our problem. Completing an IRA rollover is a nontaxable event, meaning no income tax is due AND you avoid the 10% early withdrawal penalty. Requesting a full liquidation directly from your plan puts you in the jeopardy box right out of the gate. By law, the plan is required to withhold 20% from your distribution and send it to the IRS as a credit toward any tax and penalties you may owe. Ok, so how many of you pay your bills early? I did not ask if you pay them on time. I asked if you pay them early. Not you? Me neither!

Now, if on the other hand, you complete a rollover to an IRA and then request a liquidation of that IRA, you can instruct them to not withhold income tax from your distribution. That is not to say you will not owe income tax and an early withdrawal penalty on this money. What it does is give you access to 100% of your account balance less any matching contribution that has not yet vested. Any tax or penalty that may be assessed is not due and payable until next year's tax filling deadline. In this second option, you maintain control of all of your money until taxes, if any, are due.

For example, if you normally receive an income-tax refund, your refund might not be as big next year because of liquidating the IRA early. I don't see any reason to lose access to 20% of your money for up to 18 months only for the IRS to return all or a portion of it to you with no interest. Think about that. When you over pay your taxes, you are giving the IRS interest-free loans for up to 18 months, sometimes longer! Do note, depending upon where your IRA is held, you may be subject to an account termination fee if you elect this option. The standard termination fee as of the writing of this book is $75.

If you are 55 years old and want to liquidate all or a portion of your 401(k), you may be able to do so without paying the 10% early withdrawal penalty. You don't hear much about this provision. I wonder why? You must terminate employment no earlier than the year in which you turn age 55. If you retire at 54, and wait until age 55 to take a withdrawal, this provision will not apply and you will be subject to a 10% early withdrawal penalty. This provision requires separation of service. Who wants to leave a job during their peak earning years just so they can access their 401(k) savings? Absolutely no one! It is worth noting here that if you do retire between the ages of 55 and 59½ and want access to all or a portion of your 401(k) money, it may be advantageous to leave the funds in the plan (even with the higher fees). Remember, if you withdraw funds from an IRA rollover before age 59½, you pay a 10% early withdrawal penalty, whereas this provision allows you access to your account with no early withdrawal penalty as early as age 55, saving 10% of the amount withdrawn.

Last, but certainly not least, you may want to consider an in-service distribution. An in-service distribution simply involves moving your money at any age to a different plan (like an IRA) while still working. Don't get too excited. In-service distributions are rare and not all plans allow them. If you determine that in service withdrawals are permitted within your plan, you would simply follow the course of action mentioned earlier to roll the desired amount to an IRA and then request a liquidation from there.

With our future contributions stopped and a goal to liquidate the money we already have in the plan as soon as possible, we are well on our way to diffusing this ticking tax bomb! Now, you are probably wondering what to do with the money you withdraw from your 401(k)? Don't worry. I'm not gonna leave ya hangin'. I've got an idea in mind that might turn this mess around. I just want to share a couple more things with you first.

Chapter 7 |
Is There Light at the End of the Tunnel?

As a kid, I loved to watch cartoons. One of my favorites was "Road Runner" (Beep! Beep!). You remember Wile E. Coyote? He was always trying to out-smart the Road Runner. In each episode, instead of animal senses and cunning, the Coyote used complicated contraptions and elaborate plans to pursue the Road Runner. The Coyote often obtains complex and ludicrous devices from a mail-order company, the fictitious "Acme Corporation," which he hopes will help him catch the Road Runner. The devices invariably fail in improbable and spectacular ways. Whether this is a result of operator error or faulty merchandise is debatable. The Coyote usually ends up burnt to a crisp, squashed flat, at the bottom of a canyon or some combination of the three. Occasionally, Acme products do work quite well. In this case, their success often works against the Coyote. Other times he uses items that are implausible, such as a superhero outfit, thinking he could fly wearing it, only to discover he can't.

In the spirit of the Coyote, I am diligently looking for a retirement planning vehicle that will defeat the IRS (Beep! Beep!).

One of the newer retirement planning products is the Roth IRA. Roth IRAs have gained popularity in recent years. They've been more popular with younger investors, who tend to be in lower tax brackets.

With a Roth IRA, you pay the income tax upfront. That means your withdrawals are tax-free so long as the account has been open five years and you are at least 59½ years old. Wow, this sounds like a winner!

To fully understand how this product works, I decided to conduct a case study on a 28-year-old male with current living expenses of $56,500. Let's call him "Wiley." He opens a Roth IRA and contributes $5,500 every year (the maximum for 2013-2014). The investment vehicle for the account is mutual funds. He desires to retire at age 58 and maintain his current lifestyle. Will he reach his goal?

Inflation has averaged 3.22% since 1913. To maintain purchasing power, Wiley will need $151,381.05 per year at age 58 to maintain his lifestyle. The Roth IRA will need to support annual distributions of $151,381.05 from age 58 to age 82 (the life expectancy of a 28-year-old male, according to the Social Security Administration). Assuming his mutual funds average 7% (which we now know is nearly impossible to do with an investment that goes up AND down), Wiley will need to contribute $480,000 over the next 30 years. If his funds average less than 7%, Wiley will have to save even more! Assuming the contribution limits for the Roth IRA remain at $5,500 per year, Wiley will only be able to contribute a total of $165,000 ($5,500 x 30). This represents a shortfall of 65.6%. I suppose it is entirely possible that the IRS could raise the contribution limit from $5,500 to $16,000 per year beginning in 2015, but it's highly unlikely.

Next, I turned my attention to the income limitations on Roth IRAs. In 2014, contributions for single filers begin to phase out at $114,000. This means if Wiley makes more than $114,000 he is not allowed to contribute the full $5,500 to his Roth IRA and if he earns more than $129,000 he cannot contribute ANY money to his Roth IRA. As Wiley's earning potential grows, he may find that he is no longer eligible to make contributions to his Roth IRA. That's unfortunate. If Wiley is making $129,000 a year he can afford to save some serious money for retirement. With these restrictions, it's safe to say it won't be in his Roth IRA.

On a positive note, the Roth IRA has some unique liquidity

provisions prior to retirement, making this savings vehicle more attractive to young investors. For example, Wiley can withdrawal his contributions at ANY time income-tax and penalty-free. Remember, he has already paid income tax on his contributions, so he can have those back any time he wants or needs them.

I know several people who have used their Roth IRA as their emergency fund. Investor beware! Yes, you may access your contributions at any time for any reason but you will NEVER be allowed to "redeposit" those funds into your account, jeopardizing your dreams of retirement. Wouldn't it be nice though if we COULD withdraw funds, say to send a child to college and then deposit them back into our account? Now I'm dreaming!

Imagine the following chain of events. Today the market drops 50%. Tomorrow the market gains 50%. The next morning the headline of the Wall Street headlines would read: "Market Recovers From Violent Two-Day Swing." After all, if it's down 50% and up 50% the average return would be 0% for that two day period (+50 -50 = 0/2 = 0). Right? Do another exercise with me. Today, I have $100 and lose 50%. I have $50 at the end of the day. Tomorrow I gain 50%. I have $75 at the end of day two ($50 x 50% = $25 + $50 = $75). Your investment did NOT recover. You are down $25 or 25%! Roth IRAs may avoid income tax, but they sure don't avoid market volatility when invested in a variable product.

Let's assume for a moment there are no contribution limits, no income limits and no liquidity issues. Wiley is able to contribute the $480,000 over the next 30 years and the market averages 7% each and every year. The ONLY way Wiley will attain his retirement goal is if the market never has a negative day. That's right. Not one single negative day. Why? Because as we've already learned, when the market goes down, you step in a big hole. The bigger that hole, the longer it takes to get out of it. Roth IRAs invested in a variable investment such as mutual funds provide absolutely NO guarantees.

Wiley desires to retire at age 58. Can a tax-free withdrawal be taken from a Roth IRA at age 58? The answer is "no." With a few exceptions, the account must be opened for a minimum of five years AND the client must be 59½ years of age or older. Although the Roth IRA has no requirement to withdraw money at age 70½ like the Traditional IRA does, withdrawals are restricted until both requirements have been met.

I think it's pretty clear, Wiley will not be able to attain his retirement goal utilizing the Roth IRA as we know it today. Now, I know what you're thinking. Wiley can overcome the $5,500 annual contribution limit by contributing his money to a Roth 401(k) instead of the Roth IRA. Yes. The Roth 401(k) is another option although it is not available to everyone. Let's take a look.

Since Jan. 1, 2006, U.S. employers have been allowed to amend their 401(k) plan document to allow employees to elect "Roth IRA type" tax treatment for a portion or all of their contributions. The Roth 401(k) combines some of the most advantageous aspects of both the 401(k) and the Roth IRA. Under the Roth 401(k), employees may contribute funds on an after-tax basis instead of a pre-tax basis. Employers are permitted to make matching contributions on employees' designated Roth contributions. However, employers' contributions CANNOT receive the Roth tax treatment. The matching contributions made on account of designated Roth contributions must be allocated to a pre-tax account, just like traditional 401(k) contributions. Contribution limits for Roth 401(k) plans are the same as those for traditional 401(k) plans. Additional administrative recordkeeping and payroll processing is causing the adoption of these plans to be relatively slow.

With a Roth 401(k), Wiley would be able to contribute up to $17,500 per year resolving the Roth IRA contribution limit issue but would take on the burden of the annual fee, which as we discussed earlier was as high as 3.34% in 2012 for some plans. The Roth 401(k) does nothing for the income limitations ($114,000 and $129,000 for a single filer in 2014), market volatility, the fact there are no guarantees and retirement prior to age 59 ½ is prohibited if you want to receive tax-free income. So, is this a good alternative?

If you don't mind being subject to the wiles of the market and being told when you can and cannot have your money, then you might be inclined to settle for this option. Personally, I don't like losing money and I want access to MY MONEY when I want MY MONEY!

I think the Roth IRA is a bit of a teaser. Did you really believe the IRS would let you accumulate hundreds of thousands of dollars in a retirement account and never collect a dime of income tax on it? Come on! Using a Roth IRA as your only strategy to fund your retirement dreams is like trying to put a Band-Aid on a gaping wound … it's a temporary fix, if that. I'm going to dig a little deeper and see what else might be out there.

Alas, the light at the end of the tunnel is not what it seems.

Turns out, it's just Road Runner with a flashlight attached to his head.

PART 2
ORMAN'S "INVESTMENT HATE LIST"

Chapter 8 | Annuities Are NOT Bad Investments

Here's Suze Orman's "Investment Hate List," according to "The Laws of Money – 5 Timeless Secrets to Get Out and Stay Out of Financial Trouble," 2003.

1. No variable annuities, especially in a retirement account
2. No whole life insurance policies
3. No universal life insurance policies
4. No variable universal life insurance policies
5. No mutual funds that carry a load (A or B shares)
6. No bond funds (especially intermediate or long-term)

How many of you remember the first cell phone? In October 1983, the phone resembled a brick. Back then, the phone cost $3,900. This is like buying a phone today for $10,000! Geez, that's expensive.

There are countless phones available today; each model a little different than the next and priced accordingly. We all know there are some phones that are better than others and there are certain manufacturers who have experienced difficulty with their products some of which are no longer in business today. We also know that the majority of these phones come with strict contracts, including steep charges if you go over your allotted minutes and high dollar cancellation fees should you decide Verizon has better coverage in your area than AT&T. Guess what? That does not mean the cell phone is a bad product or that you should never own one!

So let's use the phone as an analogy when looking at annuities. An annuity is a tool designed to do a very specific thing: Provide guaranteed income. Much like the cell phone that now does so much more than make a phone call, an annuity has evolved over the years to include features that were not even dreamed about when it was first introduced.

Now let's look at some examples of how an annuity works. How do you think a professional athlete's contract is funded? You guessed it! An annuity. Currently, Alex Rodriguez is in a 10-year contract with the New York Yankees for $27,500,000 per year. That contract is worth $275 million dollars! Do you think that the Yankees put $275,000,000 in a savings account with A-Rod's name on it? I seriously doubt it. A better idea would be to have an insurance company using current interest rates calculate an amount needed today that would increase over time to an amount that would pay the entire $275,000,000 over a 10-year period. Once that amount has been determined and deposited with that insurance company, it is now the company's responsibility to write a check for $27,500,000 every year. The value of an annuity lies in transferring risk.

Ok, here's another example. Do you know anyone who has won the lottery? I do. Jackpot winners have the option of receiving their prize in cash or as a graduated annuity paid in 30 yearly installments. The advertised estimated jackpot represents the total payments that would be paid to a jackpot winner should they accept the 30-installment option. If the winner elects the cash option, he receives considerably less.

So why are there so many "annuity haters"? Most people are biased toward whatever they are most familiar with, and for the most part do not have malicious intentions. Ken Fisher is currently running the following ad: "I HATE annuities and you should, too." From what I have read, most people who trash-talk annuities have three main beefs: Commissions, expenses and taxation. Annuity commissions can range from 1-10%. In comparison, real estate agents are paid 6% to sell your home and nobody is burning them at the stake! It's also worth noting here that Ken Fisher was listed on the 2013 Forbes 400 list of richest Americans and Forbes list of world billionaires with a net worth of $2.3B (that's billion with a "B"). He is a self-made billionaire and his source of wealth is money management. He currently has $50 billion in assets under management and has been called the largest wealth manager in the United States. In comparison, the average advisory fee is 1% ANNUALLY. So, if you were to allow a Money Manager to manage your money say for the next 25 years while you are in retirement, you would pay 25% in total commission. Actually, they don't like the word commission, so they call it "fees." Call it what you like. I've searched far and wide and cannot find any articles trash-talking money managers for charging excessive commissions — I mean fees.

Here's the bottom line. Commission should NOT be a factor. You need to focus on what the annuity does for you. Not what it does for the advisor! Transferring the risk of possibly running out of money during retirement can be extremely valuable.

Now, when it comes to expenses, annuities are no different than a new automobile. You can get one that gets the job done or you can get one that is loaded to the hilt. If you opt for the loaded version, it's gonna cost ya. And yes, taxation on an annuity is different than taxation on other investments. That being said, it is still very wrong to lump all annuities into one category and say they are bad.

In my quest to peel back the layers of these controversial products, I discovered a number of features that the "haters" have failed to mention. Although this chapter is not intended to be your complete resource for annuities, I do want to discuss the basic types of annuities, how they work, their features and liquidity.

First, an annuity contract is created when an individual pays a life insurance company a single premium that will later be distributed back to the insured party over time. Remember, the sole purpose of this investment tool is to provide guaranteed income.

Annuities have two phases: The accumulation phase and the distribution phase. If you have no intention of utilizing the distribution phase, this product is not for you. Due to the taxation on this product (all earnings are taxed as ordinary income), this is not the best place to accumulate money and then take a lump-sum distribution.

Types of annuities

Annuities are a tax-deferred vehicle, meaning you pay no tax on the monies earned inside the annuity until withdrawn. We've already discussed how dangerous tax-deferral can be so I need you to keep that in mind as we dig into this product. Annuities can be broken down into three categories (technically two): Fixed, variable and equity indexed, which is a type of fixed annuity.

The fixed annuity can be compared to a certificate of deposit in that you deposit a sum of money with an insurance company for a fixed period of time. The insurance company agrees to pay you a fixed rate of interest while they have your money on deposit and to return your principal at the end of the term. The industry refers to this as a MYGA, Multi-Year Guaranteed Annuity. Seems easy enough, except in recent years it has become difficult to get a fixed rate for the entire term. It seems more and more carriers want to offer what I call a "teaser" rate for the first year or two. For example, one insurance company offers an annuity whose current declared interest rate (3.5%) is guaranteed for the first two years on the initial premium submitted. After the second year, the interest rate is declared annually never to go below a base rate of 1.5%. Now your first thought might be with interest rates as low as they are, this is an opportunity for my rate to go up after 2 years. That is a possibility. But more times than not, I have seen these types of contracts go to the minimum guaranteed rate and stay there for the remainder of the term. Does this make annuities a bad investment? Absolutely not. As I've said before, if you know the rules, you can play the game. If you want to reccive a fixed rate for the entire term of your contract, simply avoid those contracts that offer teaser rates.

The variable annuity was first introduced to the United States in 1952 by TIAA-CREF (Teachers Insurance and Annuities Association – College Retirement Equity Fund). It has an investment component and an insurance component. Basically, you could now purchase your favorite mutual fund or funds with a tax-deferred wrapper. But wait, we already can do that in our 401(k) and IRA. So what gives? Some would argue that if you have max-funded your 401(k) and an IRA the variable annuity would be another tool to shelter money from taxes (remember we have already determined this is NOT a good idea). If a mutual fund, which is technically called a "subaccount," is the investment component, what is the insurance component? The insurance company plays several roles but for this discussion, it insures the principal to the beneficiary. The basic death benefit provides your beneficiaries with the greater of your purchase payments (premiums) less proportional withdrawals or your value in the annuity at time of death. In the event your variable annuity performs poorly, the insurance company has to make good on the account. This is a risk they do not take lightly. As a result, variable annuities carry a mortality and expense (M&E) charge. The average M&E charge is 1.25% and is charged annually. This expense does not apply to a fixed annuity.

Others would argue that the subaccounts inside variable annuities perform better than their "sister funds." The "sister fund" is the actual mutual fund the subaccount mimics. By design, subaccounts have the exact same holdings as their sister fund. That being the case, how would a subaccount outperform its sister fund? By definition, mutual funds (the sister fund) have to distribute at least 95% of all capital gains by calendar year-end. We need to review a small detail about mutual funds. If the market takes a nose-dive, causing investors to get nervous, they are likely to sell shares of a mutual fund to protect themselves from further losses. If the liquidation requests exceed the amount of cash the fund manager has on hand, she will be forced to sell shares of stocks and/ or bonds to raise cash. In this scenario, shares are often sold at a loss, affecting the overall performance of the fund.

One key difference between mutual funds and annuities is that investors view annuities as more of a long-term investment. Given the same scenario, this investor is likely to ride it out. The fund manager is not forced to sell to cover liquidation requests, resulting in less turnover. This not only reduces trading costs but also has been shown to improve overall performance. Interesting to know.

Thus far we have learned that a fixed annuity receives a rate of interest declared by the insurance company, whereas a variable annuity's performance can go up OR down depending upon the performance of the subaccounts you and/or your advisor choose. An insurance agent does not have to have a securities license to offer you a fixed annuity. On the other hand, variable annuities are considered to be a security and are regulated by FINRA. Only agents who are both insurance and securities licensed can offer variable annuities.

Earlier I mentioned there are technically only two categories of annuities, fixed and variable. That's because equity indexed annuities (EIAs) are a type of fixed annuity. One way to describe an indexed annuity is it is a product that let's you have your cake and eat it, too. If the market goes up, your account value goes up. If the market goes down, you can't lose. What? That's nothing short of amazing! I know, right?! Okay. So what's the catch? These annuities are often referred to as hybrids because much like a fixed annuity, you can allocate a portion of your premium to a declared rate option. You can also choose to allocate up to 100% of your premium to an option that considers the performance of a stock index such as the S&P 500 to determine how much your account is credited at the end of the term (acting a little like a variable annuity). Since the money is never invested in the stock market, the account value will never go down due to market volatility. In years where the S&P 500 loses money, the account is credited with zero. Currently, there is an annuity company with a marketing piece titled "Zero is Your Hero." I am inclined to agree!

Now, you might be wondering how this is even possible. First, we need to understand a few terms like participation rate. A participation rate will tell you how much of the gain you get to "participate" in. For example, an 80% participation rate tells me if the S&P 500 increases by 10%, my account would receive 80% of that or 8%. When this type of annuity was first introduced, participation rates were much more of a factor than they are today with the vast majority of new equity indexed annuities offering a 100% participation rate. Before you go and move all of your money into one of these guys, we need to understand cap rate. A cap rate, well … caps your rate — ha! In other words, there is a limit to the amount of the gain you get to keep. In our example above, if the cap rate were 4% your account would be credited with 4% at the end of the term instead of 8%. I have to admit, I am very intrigued by this "Zero Is Your Hero" strategy and you should be, too! For now, let's continue our discussion of annuities. In Chapter 10, I will explain exactly how this new strategy, aka Indexing works.

So you own an annuity. How do you get your money out? Remember, the sole purpose of this investment tool is to provide guaranteed income. If you do not intend to utilize the distribution phase of an annuity, you should probably consider another investment option. When you enter the distribution phase of your contract, you will have a decision to make. You will either annuitize your contract or take systematic withdrawals. SIT UP AND PAY ATTENTION. Annuitizing your contract is PERMANENT. I'm already getting nervous just thinking about it.

How many of you know someone who retired with an option to take their pension in a lump sum OR a monthly check for the rest of their life? When you give an insurance company a lump sum of money in exchange for a guaranteed stream of income for the rest of your life, you have annuitized your asset. This decision is irrevocable; you cannot change it no matter how hard you try. If that retiree elected the monthly check, the company took the lump sum that was previously offered to the retiree and sent it to an annuity company (they transferred the risk). The insurance company is now responsible for sending the retiree a monthly check (just like A-Rod). There's a little bit more to it though.

The retiree also has to decide if he wants a life only or joint life payout. I HIGHLY ADVISE AGAINST A LIFE-ONLY PAYOUT. Think about it. Retirement arrives. You decide a monthly check is the best option for you and your family. The joint life payout was less than the life only payout so you elected life only. Before your first check arrives, you are in a fatal car accident. YOUR ONLY LIFE JUST ENDED! The insurance company will keep every dime of your retirement and pay your family nothing.

Does this make an annuity a bad investment? Absolutely not! If we know the rules, we can play the game. If on the other hand, you had elected the joint life payout, you would receive a slightly smaller monthly check, but that check will be paid until both you and your spouse are dead. Now, what if both you and your spouse were in the car at the time of the accident and there were no survivors? The insurance company will keep EVERY DIME of your retirement and pay your family nothing. Good Lord! I'm beginning to think annuities are a bad investment ... just kidding!

This brings us to an option known as "period certain." This option provides income for a guaranteed period. Life with 10-year period certain is one option. If you die five years after you begin collecting, the payments continue to your survivor for five more years. Most companies go as high as 20-year period certain. Please understand, your age and length of guarantee affect the amount of your check. With this option, you can rest assured someone you love will receive your hard earned dollars.

I have a confession. I have a hard time recommending to anyone to annuitize a contract. Why? Because you don't have to annuitize your contract in order to receive monthly income.

You're looking at your retirement printout and see that the life-only option produces $1,800 monthly. You can take the lump-sum option, roll it into an annuity and begin taking systematic withdrawals of $1,800 every month. I like to think of a systematic withdrawal like a faucet. If you need income, you turn it on. If you need more income, you turn the faucet up a little bit, and if you hit the lottery and no longer need the income, you turn the faucet off! A couple of things to keep in mind here is that once you annuitize, the monthly amount is fixed in stone. You will get that check whether you need it or not and if your expenses increase (and they will) you cannot increase the amount of your check.

In addition, you pay ordinary income tax on every check you receive. By utilizing systematic withdrawals, you can control your income tax by deciding when and when not to take withdrawals. No doubt you are starting to appreciate the flexibility of systematic withdrawals over rigid annuitization.

By electing to roll your lump sum into an annuity and take systematic withdrawals, you are shouldering the risk of running out of money while you are in retirement.

If this makes you uncomfortable, you can utilize a feature that most of the annuity haters fail to mention. In my professional opinion, these features are what make an annuity a valuable retirement option. I am talking about income riders.

Now, if acronyms frighten you, prepare to be terrified! It's true. Income riders can be confusing, but they do not have to be. Income riders give you the benefit of a guaranteed income for life without forcing you to annuitize your contract. Hey, I like that! These riders are OPTIONAL on both variable and indexed annuities and ARE NOT FREE.

Income riders were first made available on variable annuities. The best way for me to explain a variable annuity with an income rider is to ask you to take out a sheet of paper and draw a line down the middle creating two columns. Your "account values" are on the left. Your "living benefits" are on right. In the left column, jot down these three terms: Account value, surrender value and death benefit. We already have discussed that the value of a variable annuity can go up AND down. Thus, when you receive your statement, the account value will be worth more or less than your initial premium. It's that simple. The next number that usually jumps off the page is your surrender value, which I like to call your "walk-away number." If you are in the initial years of your contract, the surrender value will always be worth less than the account value, but may be more than your initial premium. At some point, your account value and surrender value will be equal, which means your surrender period has ended. If you purchased an annuity and have now decided to cash out instead of receiving a lifetime income, this is your number (stay tuned for more on surrender charges when we discuss liquidity). The death benefit seems rather self-explanatory. It is the amount your beneficiary will receive at your death. The GMDB (guaranteed minimum death benefit) will equal your account value unless your contract has performed poorly, and if so, it will be no less than the total of your premiums adjusted for any withdrawals. Some variable annuities offer an enhanced guaranteed minimum death benefit. This feature locks in gains within the contract on every anniversary date to the beneficiary. Your left column is now complete.

In the right column, list the following: GMAB and GLWB. If you're getting the least bit drowsy, go grab a cup of coffee before proceeding. Yes, we have more acronyms and lots of them. First, let me be clear. Let me be VERY clear. You will never receive ANY of the numbers on the right side of your paper in a lump sum. We are about to discuss OPTIONAL living benefits available to you for an ADDITIONAL charge.

Think of the last new car you purchased. There were some things you absolutely had to have and then there were some options you selected because they provided an added value. These riders are no different.

Have you ever heard of an annuity that is guaranteed to increase 7% every year? What about unicorns? Have you heard about them? Sure you have but they don't exist and neither do annuities that are guaranteed to increase 7% every year. So why in the world would your advisor tell you that? Your advisor is describing a GMAB, guaranteed minimum accumulation benefit, and doing a poor job I might add.

So what is it and what can it do for you? Keeping in mind the value of a variable annuity can go up AND down, this is a way to guarantee you have a certain dollar amount in the future to base your lifetime income benefit on. If you invest $250,000 hoping it grows to $500,000 over 10 years in order to receive $25,000/year in income (5%) for the rest of your life but end up with about $260,000, you are either going to have to work longer or live on less. By the way, if you had invested at the beginning of 2000 and were planning to retire in 2010, this is exactly what would have happened. If you had a GMAB that was guaranteed to increase by 7% every year, you would in fact have a $500,000 accumulation benefit. Can you liquidate your annuity and get a check for $500,000? NO! Why? Because. Your "walk-away number" is $260,000.

Let's stop here for a minute. Variable annuities are Suze Orman's No. 1 gripe, especially in a retirement account. Let me remind you why you purchase an annuity — to provide a guaranteed income. You do not purchase an annuity for the sole purpose of tax-deferral, although that is a benefit of how the product is structured. Orman's problem with variable annuities within a retirement account is that tax-deferral is an inherent benefit of an IRA therefore an annuity cannot provide a benefit inside an IRA. On page 509 of her book "The Road To Wealth," she responds to the following question: I'm considering buying a variable annuity to hold in my retirement account. Is this a good idea? "No! As a rule, buying any annuity to hold in a retirement account is a bad idea, and a variable annuity is no exception. The problem, in a nutshell, is this: You are buying a tax-deferred investment product to hold within a tax-deferred investment account, and so you are paying for the benefit of an extra layer of tax protection that you don't need." Wow. She has completely missed the value of these optional riders.

I will agree you are paying for a benefit but it is not the benefit of tax-deferral. You are paying for the benefit of guaranteed income. Or are you? For the sake of this discussion, let's assume you invested $250,000 in a variable annuity and added the GMAB for which the insurance company charges 1% annually. Watch what happens.

ACCOUNT VALUE	LIVING BENEFITS
$250,000	$250,000
- 2,500 (1%)	+17,500 (7%)
$247,000	$267,500

Did you see that? The additional fee for the rider is very real, but it is deducted from your account value or your "walk-away number." It is not deducted from your living benefit. Why? Because the living benefit is merely a calculation it is not actual money. The only money available to deduct a fee from is the account value. Is that important? Only if you plan to walk away. Did you get that? If you purchased this annuity to guarantee the highest income possible during your retirement years then the additional cost of this rider is a moot point in my book. I would much rather receive 5% of $267,500 than 5% of $247,000. Now you're worried that you won't have anything to leave to your beneficiary. Really?! If you specifically want to leave money to a beneficiary, do NOT invest that money into an annuity. There is a much better alternative, which we will discuss in a later chapter.

Next we come to GLWB or guaranteed lifetime withdrawal benefit. The GLWB guarantees you can withdraw a minimum amount throughout your lifetime regardless of the performance of the subaccounts AND as mentioned before you do not have to annuitize your contract to get it. The guarantee is a set percentage of your investment, which increases the longer you delay taking payments. These are referred to as age-bands and range from 4-8% depending upon your age at the time you begin receiving your income NOT your age at the time you purchase the annuity. If the value of the account goes up while you are waiting to take your payments, your income may actually increase. Hmmm ... is it possible to combine the GMAB and GLWB in the same contract? Yes, it is. Are annuities a bad investment? No. They are not.

Since the premiums deposited into an Indexed Annuity are never invested in the stock market thus avoiding losses due to market volatility, the GMAB which restores the annuity's accumulation value to the total premiums paid, should the subaccounts perform poorly is not necessary. However, the Guaranteed Lifetime Withdrawal Benefit is quite another story. Remember, it allows you to receive an annual income for life without having to annuitize your contract, an irrevocable decision. No doubt these riders vary from one carrier to the next but I came across two in particular I believe are well worth discussing here.

First, there is a carrier offering an income rider that "grows" your Living Benefits by combining a "fixed" increase with a portion of your market gains. As of the writing of this book, the minimum fixed rate is 3% with no limit on the market gain (aka Cap). Granted in a bear market where there would be no market gain, the GLWB on a variable annuity with a 7% fixed increase would certainly outperform the income rider on the indexed annuity discussed here. But, in a bull market the GLWB on this indexed annuity has unlimited potential to outperform due to the fact there is no cap on the market gain. At this point in my research, I can see value in both the variable annuity income rider AND the indexed annuity income rider. A retiree who wanted to cover all their bases might want to consider using both. But wait, there's more!

This particular carrier takes the income rider on their indexed annuity to a whole new level. With certain limitations and conditions, your guaranteed lifetime income will DOUBLE in the event you are unable to take care of yourself. What? Yes! If a doctor certifies that you are unable to complete 2 of the 6 Activities of Daily Living (ADLs) the "double" is triggered. Let me break that down a little further for you.

Long-term care is a very REAL threat to your retirement. It includes a variety of services (both medical and nonmedical) for people with a chronic illness or disability who cannot care for themselves. A study by the U.S. Department of Health and Human Services says that 4 out of every 10 people who reach age 65 will enter a nursing home at some point in their lives. About 10 percent of the people who enter a nursing home will stay there five years or more. In 2014, the average annual cost of nursing home care in the United States was $$83,950 for a semi-private room. The average annual cost for an assisted living facility was $36,000 and home health aides were paid on average $19 per hour. The average cost of a nursing home for one year is more than the typical family has saved for retirement in a 401(k) or an IRA!

To guard against this financial threat you can purchase long-term care insurance. Private long-term care insurance has grown in popularity however premiums have risen dramatically in recent years. The longer you wait to purchase coverage, the more expense the policy becomes. The most common policy requires that a person be unable to perform 2 or more activities of daily living which include eating, dressing, bathing, transferring, toileting and continence without substantial assistance OR they need substantial assistance due to a severe cognitive impairment. In either case a doctor must provide a plan of care in order to receive your benefits. It's worth noting here that you must apply and qualify for this insurance. Your premiums are based upon your age and health at time of application. Keep in mind they are not concerned with health conditions that are likely to kill you. They are terrified you will live forever and need help doing it. For example, if you have been issued a handicap-parking permit, you will probably be denied coverage. Yikes!

What if you do obtain coverage but never need it? Much like auto and homeowners insurance, if you never file a claim you do not receive any financial benefit from the policy. There is a "return of premium" rider you can add to these policies that pays all premiums back to your estate if you do not use the coverage. This rider increases the premiums substantially making it cost prohibitive.

So, we have an income rider available on an indexed annuity that includes a benefit that will DOUBLE your guaranteed lifetime income should you need long-term care. That little nugget was well worth my time to uncover! We need to stop again for a moment.

Unlike annuities, Suze is a fan of Long-Term Care Insurance. In her book The Road To Wealth she writes "For a society that's growing older by the minute, we're not providing very well for our old age. We expect individuals and families to do it mostly on their own. But even as individuals and families, we seem to be in denial about what's happening to us. Nowhere is this more obvious than with respect to long-term care insurance-perhaps the most essential king of insurance–which many of us will need when we are old. Long-term care will be a fact of life for most of us, so let's face it here and now. Having done so, you will, I hope, go on to buy this kind of protection." As cautious as Suze is about overpaying for anything, I have to admit I'm surprised she has overlooked the LTC benefits that are available in today's income riders. For one, it is a fringe benefit of a product that does other things you need during retirement, aka guaranteed income for life. Two, there is no medical qualifying. THAT IS HUGE! What if you already have a handicap-parking permit? Just kidding. But seriously, think of how many people get to retirement without purchasing long-term care insurance only to learn that either they are uninsurable or it is so expensive they cannot afford it. The income rider on this indexed annuity is worth every dime and then some.

As I mentioned, there are two different types of income riders available on indexed annuities that I want to discuss with you. The second one is quite unique and may just be my favorite. This rider was designed to be less complex than standard income riders. Where other riders have rollup rates, income account values, payout factors, restart provisions, etc., this rider focuses on clarity and simplicity. Similar to a statement of benefits provided by a defined benefit plan, the insurance company determines the income payments that you are guaranteed and then provides these amounts to you on a simple Statement of Benefits each year. If you are close to retirement you can opt for the basic rider where your benefit is determined at application and will never change. If you have a few years until retirement you may want to consider the "Plus" version of this rider. The initial benefit will be lower than if you had selected the basic rider BUT prior to receiving income, interest credited to the base annuity will increase the Lifetime Income Benefit by the same percentage as the interest credit. With the "Plus" version the Statement of Benefits is updated annually to reflect any increases to the Lifetime Income Benefit due to interest credits. Very nice!

Now, you're probably thinking that sounds good and all but wondering why this particular rider is currently my favorite? Great question and I'm so glad you asked! When you purchase the Basic or Plus version of this particular rider, not only do you get access to a guaranteed stream of income, you also get peace of mind knowing that if you require qualified care in a nursing, hospital or hospice facility you will have access to TRIPLE your Lifetime Income Benefit for up to 60 months! Oh my goodness, we know how important it is to prepare for long-term care expenses. We also know you have to medically qualify, the premiums can be expensive and if you don't use it you lose it. Although a doctor has to recommend care in writing to begin receiving benefits, there is no other medical requirement other than not being confined at the time you apply for the annuity. Easy enough! Although there is a 2-year waiting period, there are no expensive monthly premiums to pay for this LTC benefit. Yes! And if you happen to be one of the lucky ones who pass from this life into the next with no need for LTC, you didn't pay for something you never used! I love it! There is even coverage for a spouse under certain circumstances. That's just too much, but I'll take it!!

I would be remiss if I did not address the liquidity of these products. Annuities are not savings accounts. This is not where you should invest your rainy-day fund. Remember annuities are designed to do one thing; provide guaranteed income. For the most part, annuities are a retirement planning tool and as such are long-term investments.

Have you ever noticed when you purchase an annuity you are not charged a commission? Remember, there are no free lunches. If you do not pay a commission, you pay with time. Time?

Remember when bank CDs were all the rage? You would go to your local branch, deposit $100,000 for five years and the bank would pay you 6% interest (those were the days!). In exchange for keeping money on deposit for the agreed-upon term, banks usually pay higher interest rates than they do on accounts from which money can be withdrawn on demand; a savings account for example. What happens if you want your money before the 5th year is over? Withdrawals before maturity are usually subject to a substantial penalty. For a five-year CD, this is often the loss of six months' interest. So see, you already have a basic understanding of a surrender period and for the most part, you are ok with it. Why? Because you would never tie up all of your money for a long period of time making surrender periods much less of an issue than some people make them out to be.

Today's annuities have surrender periods that range up to 15 years. Surrender periods are there to make sure you hold up your end of the contract. Generally speaking, if you withdraw money prior to the end of the surrender period you pay a surrender charge. The surrender charge is usually a percentage of your initial premium and declines to zero by the end of the surrender period. The number one reason surrender charges are so high is to deter people from using annuities as a short-term investment.

I stumbled across this definition of a surrender period while surfing the Internet — "a surrender period is the amount of time an investor must wait until he or she can withdraw funds from an annuity without facing a penalty." This definition is misleading. It should read as follows: a surrender period is the amount of time an investor must wait until he or she can withdraw ALL OF THEIR funds from an annuity without facing a penalty. I think you will agree there is a big difference between not being able to withdraw any money and being able to withdraw some money. Every annuity I have come across (granted that is not all of them, but several) will allow you to withdraw at least 5% of your initial premium every year without incurring a surrender charge and some policies allow as much as 10% of initial premiums each year. We need to keep in mind annuities are retirement planning tools and as such we should NOT be withdrawing from these accounts. However, life happens. Which brings me to yet another feature of these investment products that I believe adds a great deal to their value.

We have already learned that our lifetime income benefit can be increased by as much as three times should we need long-term care insurance. As good as that sounds, what if it isn't enough? What if you have exhausted all of your other assets and your annuity is still in its surrender period? How much of a penalty can you expect to pay? The annuity haters want you to believe that it would be HUGE. But I have a surprise for them and for you. Your surrender charge would be ZERO. No, I am not kidding. The majority of annuity contracts being issued today have terminal and chronic illness waivers. Yes, you read that right! If you have been diagnosed with cancer and you need the money in your annuity to pay for chemo, take it! It's yours, every brown cent of it. Do you understand that if you purchased an annuity for the right reason — to provide guaranteed income — you have all the liquidity you need? I mean really think about it. Once you're in retirement, more than likely your major expenses will be health-care related. You don't know how many times I have heard "I don't want to tie my money up for very long ... I might need it ... I don't even buy green bananas anymore." Guess what? Annuities could make a great deal of sense for a portion of your retirement assets. Based upon my research thus far, there is no other investment (stocks, bonds, mutual funds) that can do what annuities can do at a time in your life when you may really need the extra help.

Before I leave this topic, I have to say how very disappointed I am with so-called "financial experts" who have trashed-talked and continue to trash-talk annuities. Shame on them! I am SO glad I decided to "raise the hood" on annuities. Do you realize that you can create your own pension with an annuity? Wow! How many people whine about not having a company pension when they retire? Create your own! In an article written in September 2013 titled "Annuities Provide a New Piece (Peace) of Mind" Economics expert Ben Stein endorses annuities. If that doesn't encourage you to at least consider them as a viable alternative maybe the fact that economist Ben Bernake, perhaps the single most influential human on earth when it comes to money, reportedly owns both fixed and variable annuities will.

I have referred to "Annuity Haters" throughout this chapter. If you fear that your financial advisor is a member of this group, there is a test you can administer. Ask him or her this magic question: "What are your thoughts about annuities?" The reason this question is magical is because they will have no clue they are being tested. If your advisor answers this question by listing the negative characteristics of an annuity without naming the type of annuity they are referring to — because we now know there are fixed, variable and indexed annuities — then they immediately fail the test. To provide an unbiased opinion, they need to be able to provide factual information. If they cannot do that, you need to find a new financial advisor. It's really that simple.

Annuities are loaded with valuable features and benefits that make sense for some people, even when they are held inside of an IRA. Sorry, Orman. Not!

Chapter 9 | We All Need Life Insurance

For those of you who have had a baby, you will remember leaving the hospital with a bag of "stuff." Trial-size package of diapers, wipes, formula, ointments, suction thingies (gross!), coupons and crumpled in the bottom of the bag was an offer from Gerber. We all know the Gerber Baby, the most recognized baby face in the world! Although cereal and baby food was the first thing that came to your mind, that's not what the offer was for at all. The offer was from the Gerber Life Insurance Co. In 1967, Gerber created the Gerber Life Insurance Co. as a subsidiary of the Gerber Products Co. Today, Gerber Life offers a full line of life insurance plans designed to help babies and their families enjoy a more secure financial future. I want to say that again. Gerber Life offers plans designed to help babies and their families enjoy a more secure financial future. Gerber gets it!

Why on earth would you buy life insurance on the life of a newborn? I have had more than one client get upset with me when I recommended doing just that. Their initial response is often, "I wouldn't dare bet on the life of my child," or, "I couldn't bear to gain from the death of my child." I am not asking you to do either. I am, however, asking you to give the gift of life insurance to your child. I worked with a woman years ago who did just that. She and her husband purchased a $250,000 permanent life insurance policy for their son when he was 2 years old. When he was ready to go to college, the cash value helped him buy a dependable used car, books and supplies. At the age of 20, her son was diagnosed with Crohn's disease; he is now uninsurable. Had his parents not made the decision to purchase a permanent life insurance policy on him at such an early age, he would have no coverage today. That may not seem like a big deal to you, but as you read and learn more about what it is, how it works and exactly what it can do for you and your family, you will discover that not having coverage is a tragedy on so many levels.

According to LIMRA's Life Insurance Barometer Study 2014, 88% of consumers agree that most people need life insurance. Many Americans have no life insurance while others don't have enough. LIMRA's study goes on to ask if life insurance can help meet many of the financial needs of consumers, what's stopping more of them from buying? Similar to the past few years, perceived expense topped the list, but nearly as many potential buyers say it's because they have other financial priorities. The second most common reason, they think they can't afford it.

I believe there is yet another reason. I believe the majority of consumers today have monstrous misconceptions about life insurance. Rather than taking time to learn about the product and how it has evolved over the years, they listen to talk-show hosts and financial celebrities who also have not taken the time to learn about the products available today yet they have been given a "stage" from which they spew their opinions all over highly impressionable consumers. Numbers 2, 3 and 4 on Orman's "Investment Hate List" involve life insurance. Rather than focusing on the many benefits of life insurance, Orman and many other financial gurus choose to rant about how much money the insurance agent makes and how expensive the policies are, advising consumers to seek out the cheapest coverage possible. How often have you tried to cut corners only to end up with something that doesn't last or doesn't work at all? Probably more times than you and I care to admit!

Let's begin with the basics. Life insurance is the foundation of EVERY financial plan. It is a contract between a policyholder and an insurer where the insurer promises to pay a designated beneficiary a sum of money upon the death of the insured person. There are many reasons to own life insurance. I encourage you to read Melissa Wandall's story at www.lifehappens.org. Melissa's husband, Mark, was a life insurance agent who not only believed in life insurance but owned it as well. Mark had no idea when he purchased his policy what it would mean to Melissa and Madison Grace, his unborn child. Less than one week after his first anniversary and 19 days before the birth of his only child, Mark was struck and killed by a driver who ran a red light. The life insurance allowed Melissa to remain in the family home, take time off from her career so she can be a full-time mom, and put money into a college fund for Madison Grace. Life insurance provided Melissa with options she would not have otherwise had.

It's clear Mark saw the value in protecting his family should the unheard of happen. How many 30-year-olds do you know who died less than a week after their first wedding anniversary and 19 days before their only child was born? Not that many, but it happened to Mark. They say the plumber's house is never plumbed. Thank goodness for Melissa her life insurance agent husband had his house in order.

Mark wanted Melissa to have enough money to pay off their debts, send their children to college and be able to maintain their overall lifestyle should he die prematurely. These are exactly the types of things people think about when they are considering the need to purchase life insurance. Here is a worksheet that can help you get a sense of how much life insurance you need to protect your family. However, you should consult with a qualified insurance professional before buying any insurance products.

See the Life Insurance Needs Worksheet on page 64.

LIFE INSURANCE NEEDS WORKSHEET

Income

1. Total annual income your family would need if you died today.
$_____

What your family needs after taxes to maintain its current standard of living (typically 60-75% of total income).

2. Annual income your family would receive from other sources.
$_____

Spouse's earnings including social security if applicable.

3. Income to be replaced. Subtract line 2 from line 1.
$_____

4. Capital needed for Income. Multiply line 3 by factor from Table 1
$_____

Expenses

5. Funeral and other final expenses.
$_____

Typically the greater of $15,000 or 4% of your estate.

6. Mortgage and other outstanding debts.
$_____

Include mortgage balance, credit card debt, car loans, etc.

7. College costs for each child, in today's dollars.
$_____

Go to http://cgi.money.cnn.com/tools/collegecost/collegecost.html to find your school and its current rates.

8. Capital needed for college.
$_____

Multiply line 7 by the appropriate factor in Table 2.

9. *Total capital required. Add lines 4, 5, 6 and 8.*

$_____

Assets

10. *Savings and investments.*

$_____

Bank accounts, money market, CDs, stocks, bonds, mutual funds, etc.

11. *Retirement savings.*

$_____

IRAs, 401(k)s, Keoghs, pension and profit-sharing plans

12. *Present amount of life insurance.*

$_____

Include group insurance as well as insurance purchased on your own.

13. *Total income-producing assets. Add lines 10, 11 and 2.*

$_____

14. *Life insurance needed. Subtract line 13 from line 9.*

$_____

Table 1		Table 2	
Years income needed	Factor	Years before college	Factor
10	8.8	5	0.95
15	12.4	10	0.91
20	15.4	15	0.86
25	18.1	20	0.82

*Note: These tables help estimate Net Present Value (NPV) the amount of capital required today to meet future income or college costs needs. The calculation assumes a 6% investment return, 3% inflation and 5% for college costs.

As you complete the worksheet something to consider is whether you want your spouse to continue working or if you want them to be able to stay home and raise your children. If you have children and opt for your spouse to continue working, you will need to factor in the expense of a nanny. Also, don't assume your child(ren) will receive a scholarship to college. If they do, great! You will have extra money to put toward your retirement. If not, you will be prepared to give them the education they need and deserve.

As we get older, our reasons for owning life insurance change. Where can you invest $500 today that will turn into $650,000 tomorrow if you get run down by a Mack truck? Ugh …Nowhere, unless you invested that $500 into a life insurance policy. It's like buying a lottery ticket where the odds of winning are 1 in 1. You play, you win! Actually, buying life insurance is better than buying a lottery ticket. Many people are unaware that life insurance pays a tax-free death benefit. Yes, you heard me right. If you are the beneficiary of a life insurance policy, the monies you receive are income tax free. Just to be clear, proceeds from a winning lottery ticket are not!

Because of the leverage and tax benefits of life insurance, many people utilize it to create wealth. There are actually two ways to create wealth with life insurance. The death benefit is the most obvious way. Some people have millions of dollars of life insurance just because they want to be sure they can leave a certain amount of money behind to their loved ones. Since there are no guarantees with stocks, bonds and mutual funds, life insurance is the easiest way to do that and I might add the fastest. You can save for years and not accumulate the kind of money a life insurance policy will pay out if you die prematurely. The second way to create wealth is by utilizing a feature within permanent life insurance called "cash value". We will discuss this feature in great detail in a later chapter but for now just know that it is possible to put "extra" money into most life insurance policies that you can access later, before you die.

There is yet another reason for owning life insurance and it is growing in popularity. Recently I heard about a doctor in south Florida who has a sign posted in his lobby that says, "I do not carry malpractice insurance." In order to see this doctor, you must sign a waiver acknowledging that you are aware he does not carry malpractice insurance. Seems a little odd on the surface but we all know malpractice insurance premiums cannot be cheap. With all of the ambulance chasers and people spilling hot coffee on themselves in drive-thrus and then suing for damages, lawsuits have gotten a little out of hand; just sayin'. Nonetheless, this doctor has decided he's not playin' that game.

You might think his actions are irresponsible. After all if he is sued and loses, the court could take everything he has! Well, not everything. Each state has its own definition of asset protection, and in Florida it includes life insurance and annuity contracts as well as your primary residence and a few other items. Here is an excerpt from the Florida statute:

Cash value in insurance and all annuities are protected from creditors' claims by Florida Statutes. While a Florida resident is alive, the cash value of any insurance policy he owns on his life or on other Florida residents is exempt from creditors claims. The protection afforded to the cash surrender value of a life insurance policy is only for the benefit of the owner/insured.

The protection of cash value insurance and annuities extends to proceeds withdrawn by the owner. Florida courts have held that funds withdrawn from a cash value insurance policy and annuity payments received by a debtor remain protected as long as the funds can be accurately traced to a bank account readily accessible to the debtor.

So what did this doctor do? Instead of wasting hundreds of thousands of dollars in malpractice insurance premiums, he bought and paid cash for a very nice home (he can access the equity should he need cash flow) and purchased life insurance policies that he regularly overfunds on himself. Overfunding is contributing far more than the cost of the insurance to his policy, which accumulates as cash value and is accessible to him during his life. Sue all you want! This doctor has protected himself by placing all of his money into assets that the state of Florida has ruled creditors cannot touch. WOW! What a plan. You don't have to be a doctor to take advantage of this idea. Let's say you have $100,000 in a bank CD and tomorrow you wreck and accidentally kill someone. They sue. They win. You can say "good-bye" to that $100,000 bank CD unless it is a protected asset, which in the state of Florida it is not. Each state has a list of assets that are protected from creditors.

The remainder of this chapter is dedicated to educating you on the evolution of life insurance, the types of coverage available today and exactly how the policies work so that you will have the information necessary to make the best decisions for you and your family.

There are numerous types of policies, but there are only two types of coverage: Permanent and term. It doesn't take a rocket scientist to figure out that one provides benefits for your entire life while the other only provides benefits for a period of time. The earliest form of permanent life insurance was offered in the 18th century as a fixed premium, fixed return product known as whole life insurance. Whole life insurance is a life insurance policy that remains in force for the insured's whole life and requires (in most cases) premiums to be paid into the policy every year. Whole life insurance premiums are the highest in the industry. Why is that? Simply put, the insurance company over-charges you on purpose. They then return the "overage" to you (if you own a participating policy) and are allowed to call it a dividend. The IRS knows it is not a dividend by definition but rather a return of your own money and thus does not charge income tax on said dividend. Why would anyone tolerate this pricing structure? For the most part, people do not realize they are being over-charged.

Let me break this down a little further. Premiums are based on several factors but basically your sex, age and the overall condition of your health determine how much the insurance company will charge to insure you. Let's assume you are 20 years old and in excellent health. The following year you maintain your health and turn 21 years old. Question: Does it cost more to insure a 20-year-old or more to insure a 21-year-old, all things being equal? The answer is it costs more to insure a 21 year old. We need to establish that the cost of insurance goes up every year because we are one year closer to death. Earlier, I told you that whole life insurance premiums are fixed. If the cost of insurance goes up every year, how can your premium remain the same? Simply put, you pay extra in the beginning. More specifically, the insurance company determines the cost to insure you at every age between the dates you apply and when the actuarial table says you will die. They total those costs and divide by your life expectancy. If a 20-year-old is expected to live to age 95, the insurer would divide the total of all the premiums from age 20 to age 95 by 75. You would then pay that amount every year until you die.

Simplified example: It costs $50 to insure a 20-year-old and $70 to insure a 21-year-old.

$$\$50 + \$70 = \$120 / 2 = \$60$$

A whole life fixed premium would be $60 for each year. You pay $10 extra in the first year. The extra is added to your cash value (the savings portion of your policy) until the following year when you pay another $60. It now costs $70 to insure you so the insurance company takes the $10 out of your cash value adds it to the $60 premium you pay in year 2 and covers the cost of your insurance.

There are some types of whole life policies whose premiums are not fixed and that are designed to be "paid-up" at a certain age. This book is not designed to educate you on every variation that exists today. When I speak of whole life policies, we will assume they are participating policies the premiums are fixed and are paid to age 100 or date of death whichever comes first.

Before we move on, it is worth noting that the "extra" money you pay in the early years of the policy does earn interest. Most policies have a guaranteed interest rate; your cash value will never earn less than this rate. However, there are aspects of the policy that are non-guaranteed. In addition, the insurance company reserves the right to change any component of the dividend scale, which will cause your policy values to change. Joseph M. Belth, a distinguished insurance professor, published "The Insurance Forum." In the March 2008 issue, he reported, "Banks disclose savings account interest calculations, and life insurance companies should disclose dividend calculations. However, companies are reluctant to reveal the information voluntarily because they fear doing so would place them at a disadvantage if their competitors do not take a similar action. State insurance regulators are responsible for the confidentiality that surrounds the determination of life insurance dividends. I believe that the regulators should require companies to make their dividend methodologies available to the public." It's hard to believe they can actually get away with this! Companies that offer whole life insurance gladly accept your money but do not have to tell you how they spend or invest it. Whole life insurance policies offer zero transparency, and if I had to guess, I would say it is not going to change any time soon.

OK. We have our first form of permanent life insurance, whole life insurance. It guarantees a death benefit as long as the premiums are paid; it is very expensive; and the insurance company does not have to tell you how your premium dollars are spent. With all of the unscrupulous activities we have witnessed in the financial services industry, I am going to go out on a limb and say that today's consumer not only prefers, but demands transparency! With that in mind, if there was a type of life insurance that provided guarantees, was less expensive and revealed where every penny of our premium dollar was spent, I believe today's consumer would want to know about it. Keep reading.

Does the name Arthur L. "Art" Williams Jr. ring a bell? He was born in Georgia, received a bachelor's degree from Mississippi State University and a master's degree from Auburn. His childhood dream was to become a professional football coach. In 1965, Williams' father suddenly died of a heart attack. He had a whole life insurance policy that left their family underinsured. Since whole life insurance premiums are expensive, people often cannot afford to purchase the amount of coverage they truly need. Five years later, his cousin introduced him to the concept of term life insurance, a much cheaper and simpler alternative to whole life, which at that time was almost never sold and rarely heard of outside the insurance industry. Williams was disturbed by the whole idea of not knowing there was a choice when buying life insurance. Believing that families were paying too much for whole life policies that left them poor in the wallet and deeply underinsured, Williams joined his cousin at ITT Financial Services in 1970. In June 1973, he left and came on board with Waddell & Reed. He did well at W&R, but it soon became clear that with a corporate structure where the executives, not the sales force, owned the company, there would be limits on how much the company could grow. On Feb. 10, 1977, A.L. Williams & Associates was founded on a simple philosophy: "Buy Term and Invest the Difference." He convinced many customers to switch from their conventional whole life insurance to term policies.

One man single-handedly changed the life insurance landscape! A.L. Williams capitalized on the fact that you could purchase term life insurance with the same death benefit as whole life insurance for much less. Why is term so much cheaper than permanent? Both term insurance and permanent insurance use the same mortality tables. Did you get that? If they are using the same mortality tables then why does one policy charge more than the other? Because permanent life insurance is based upon your life expectancy (more liability) and term insurance is based upon say the next 10 years (less liability), term insurance will always be less expensive than permanent.

Note: When the 10-year term policy expires and you choose to renew for another 10 years, you will see a significant increase in premium (the carrier's liability as increased because you are 10 years closer to death).

The other reason term insurance is less expensive is because the majority of term policies expire worthless. That means you outlive your policy. In fact, one study reported that only 1% of term insurance policies pay a benefit! The low payout likelihood (less liability) allows term insurance to be relatively inexpensive. Consumers can often purchase a term policy with up to 10 times the coverage of permanent insurance for the same premium. Or as A.L. Williams positioned it, you could purchase the same coverage and have quite a bit of money left over to invest. He built an entire career on, Buy Term and Invest the Difference.

Many financial gurus advocate A.L. Williams' strategy. On the surface it sounds good but in reality it's not at all. Yes, you can purchase more coverage for less money but what happens at the end of the term? You have three options: Drop your coverage, renew your coverage or convert your coverage if you purchased a convertible policy.

Note: If the only type of life insurance you can afford is term insurance, please be sure to purchase a term policy that is convertible to permanent insurance at a later date.

Although Orman and other financial gurus contend that you no longer need life insurance once your kids are grown, the mortgage is paid and retirement accounts are funded, we have already established that we need life insurance regardless of our age, so dropping the coverage is not an option. That leaves us with renewing or converting your coverage. With both of these options, your premium will increase. Why? Because you are closer to death, I mean you are older. Many consumers are not prepared for this when their term policies expire. Whether you are prepared or not, if you intend to keep your coverage you will pay a premium that is based upon your then current age. Level premium term life insurance is where the premium is guaranteed to be the same for a given period of time such as 10,15, 20 or 30 years. The longer the term is, the higher the premium. Most level term programs include a renewal option. It is important to note that the renewal may or may not be guaranteed and the insured should review their contract to see if evidence of insurability is required to renew the policy. You may not need to medically re-qualify but the premium for the next term (say 10 years) will be based upon your then current age. As the insured ages, the premiums increase with each renewal period. Eventually the premiums will exceed the cost of a permanent policy. By that time, you may not be able to medically qualify for a permanent policy. Which is why if you can only afford term life insurance you must purchase a policy that is convertible to permanent insurance with the same death benefit at a later date. This gives you a few years to get your financial ducks in a row. The nice thing about converting to the permanent policy is that it will be rated exactly like the original term policy. If your policy was issued when you were 20 years of age and you were rated premier plus, then your permanent policy will be rated premier plus even if you have gained weight or been diagnosed with a terminal illness. Makes you think twice about getting insurance as soon as you can! Every day you wait the risk of becoming uninsurable increases — this is a very scary thought for me and should be for you, too!

Now that we have a better understanding of term insurance let's spend just a moment on the "invest the difference" portion of A.L. Williams tagline. We only need a moment because for the most part, NOBODY DOES THIS. That's right. When you find a way to lower your phone bill by $25 each month, do you sock that $25 away in your savings account or pay $25 more toward a credit card balance? No. No, you don't. You now have the money to purchase a new pair of shoes or acrylic nails or movie tickets. None of these things are necessarily bad. My point is it takes a very disciplined person to "invest the difference" and most of us are not that disciplined. Now for those of you who are, let me remind you about the risk of the stock market and how once you "step in the hole" it is very difficult to break even, much less make a profit.

Term insurance is not the answer folks. It can, however, be used as a tool along the way as you get to where you need to be. For example, a young couple with two small children and a mortgage may need $1,000,000 or more of death benefit. Their budget may only cover $250,000 of permanent insurance. It is perfectly acceptable to purchase a convertible term policy for $750,000 of coverage that will later be converted to permanent coverage in conjunction with a $250,000 permanent life insurance policy providing the $1,000,000 of coverage the family ultimately needs.

As I said earlier, A.L. Williams single-handedly changed the landscape of the life insurance business. He and his agents successfully convinced thousands of whole life policyholders to junk their whole life insurance in exchange for term. Needless to say, the insurance industry sat up and took notice. The companies were losing market share and needed to come up with a plan to compete with the "Buy Term and Invest the Difference" movement.

Note: Never ever depend solely on group life insurance. Yes, I know it is inexpensive but if you decide to change jobs or your job is eliminated you do not take these policies with you. They do not belong to you. The "group" owns the policy and you are no longer part of the "group." This can be devastating to someone who is older and anyone who is uninsurable. Always, always, always buy individual policies. These policies belong to you and follow you wherever you go. 'Nuff said!

While A.L. Williams was blazing a path with his new philosophy, G.R. Dinney invented "The Universal Life Plan" and warned of trouble on the horizon for the insurance industry. What trouble did he foresee? Do you remember the economy of the 70s and early 80s? It was a time of poor economic performance, perhaps the worst since the great depression. With high inflation and increased unemployment, interest rates began to climb. What typically happens when interest rates increase?

So, as interest rates began to climb, people did exactly what Dinney expected them to do. They fled stocks and mutual funds and returned to bonds and savings accounts. Double-digit interest

| Bank vs. Stock Market

With so much risk in the stock market, why would anyone ever move money out of a bank and into the stock market? It's quite simple. If rates at the bank are low enough, say 1-3%, the investor is willing to take more risk to earn a higher return. The opposite is true, too. Once rates start to climb, the investor re-evaluates the risk of the stock market and will often move money back to the bank for a reasonable rate, say 3-6%, and no risk.

rates were normal by the end of the decade setting the stage for the highest interest rates in history. As you might imagine, this set off a bit of a domino effect. Not only did consumers take money out of the stock market they also borrowed money from their whole life cash value as these policies were unable to compete with even a basic savings account — wow! The insurance companies recognized they were losing a great deal of money. They had to act fast. Companies like Prudential of American, Occidental, Life of Virginia and E.F. Hutton adopted Dinney's Universal Life Plan. The product names used by these companies included Universal Life as well as others. Expanding on the "buy term and invest the difference" concept, Universal Life combines Term Life Insurance with a savings account that earns a fixed rate of interest. So what's the big deal? Well for starters, the cost of insurance for permanent insurance dropped drastically – Yay! Adding the "invest the difference" concept into the life policy, genius!

Now for some of you reading this book you may be saying, "No thanks. I'm disciplined enough to invest my difference." Good for you! But that's not why adding the savings account to the policy is genius! So what's the big deal? TAXES!! We will discuss this in detail in a later chapter. For now, I want you to think about the 1099 you received from your mutual fund last year (where you invested your difference). Some of you reinvested your dividends and did not withdraw any of your gains, yet you received a 1099! How is it possible to receive a tax bill if you didn't receive any money? Well, you can thank your neighbor, co-worker and ultimately your fund manager for that. Most mutual funds have a small cash position to cover redemption requests (what you submit when you want to withdraw some of your money). It is not uncommon, especially in volatile markets, for the redemption requests to exceed the cash on hand. When this occurs, the fund manager has no choice but to liquidate positions within the fund (shares of Wal-Mart, Apple, Coca-Cola, etc.) to create cash in order to send you the money you requested. If the shares were sold for a profit, cha-ching, taxes are due and a 1099 is generated. Do you realize that some of these positions were purchased years ago and the fund can be down for the year yet there is still a gain in the shares the fund manager sold? Let me say that differently. Do you realize you can get a tax bill even when your mutual fund loses money? Yes, it's true!

In contrast, the savings account portion of the universal life policy grows tax deferred (no 1099s) and your gains are "tax-free" if accessed properly. Now that's what I call genius! For those of you who are thinking that the small amount of income tax you have to pay each year on the 1099 you receive on your mutual fund will not make a big difference in the overall scheme of things, you're gonna want to rethink that.

So we have a term policy combined with a savings account. We all know that term insurance is cheap when you're young and gets more expensive with every passing year. The insurance company is counting on the "savings account" portion of your policy along with the interest it earns to offset the increased cost of insurance down the road. Can you see any potential problems with universal life insurance? In retrospect, there is a BIG problem.

Do you remember why this product was created? Interest rates were on the rise. By the time this product took off, interest rates were 12-15%. Why is this important? Because when an insurance company determines your premium they must make certain assumptions like the cost of insurance, which they have a handle on, and interest rates, which they don't have a handle on at all. I mean, they know what rates are today but they can't possibly know what rates will be in 20 years, right? Right! By law, they must run an illustration for you that will project the future value of your savings account and death benefit. They usually present this in a couple of different ways. First they project the value using the current interest rate and the current policy expenses. They must also show you a worse case scenario of 0% interest and the highest expenses allowed in the policy. Notice the worse case scenario always lapses (your coverage ends). We don't usually pay that much attention to the worse case scenario because the chance of interest rates going to 0% and staying there for the next 20-30 years is slim. OK. I'll buy that. But, and this is a BIG but, what are the chances that interest rates will stay at 12-15% for the next 20-30 years? Also slim and herein lies our very BIG problem. Universal life policies projected huge cash values over 20-30 years leading consumers to believe they could stop paying their premiums at certain ages and even begin to withdraw the millions of dollars that had hypothetically accumulated.

Interest rates began to fall. Cash values didn't grow as projected. Cost of insurance continued to increase. Policies were on target to lapse. Notices were mailed to policyholders. My dad was one of the policyholders who received a letter. He called his agent, a good friend of the family, and asked how could this be? His premiums weren't supposed to increase. He had three children, a wife and worked shutdowns to make ends meet. His friend began to apologize. "John, this wasn't supposed to happen. Interest rates have fallen drastically. The cost of insurance has gone up and with the loan you took against your policy there just isn't enough cash value to cover the expenses. If you don't pay the higher premiums, I'm afraid you will lose your coverage." And that he did. To add insult to injury, dad lost his coverage at an age where for him to replace the policy was cost prohibitive. My dad died in the fall of 2012. My mother did not receive any life insurance benefits.

Universal life insurance is not a bad concept. The "buy term and invest the difference" in one product allows you to take advantage of the tax benefits of a life insurance policy. The problem lies with the assumptions used in the projections. If you own a Universal Life policy, I highly recommend an insurance audit. Insurance audits evaluate your current policy to determine if you have the right type of coverage, the right amount of coverage and that you are not paying too much for that coverage.

Once again, the insurance industry found itself in a bad position. It had a good concept but when you have a fixed rate component and rates drop, you get left behind. The 1990s came and what did they bring? The dot.com era. From 1990-2000, a monkey could throw a dart and make money in the stock market. Remember what happens when rates go down? Consumers are willing to take more risk to earn more interest so they moved money back into the stock market. Universal Life was losing ground and losing ground fast. What did they do? They introduced variable universal life.

Similar to universal life, variable universal life combines term life insurance with a savings account that is invested in mutual funds instead of receiving a fixed rate. It didn't take long for that concept to catch on. The stock market was screaming and cash values were skyrocketing. Life was good ... right up until it wasn't.

It hasn't been that long ago. We all remember it and will never forget it! The period between 2000 and 2010 has become known in financial circles as "The Lost Decade." Why is that? One Hundred Thousand dollars ($100,000) invested in the S&P 500 at the beginning of 2000 was worth $104,271 at the end of 2010. For all intents and purposes, the market was flat. Now, that is ONLY true if you stayed invested and there are several of you reading this book who in fact did not! By the end of 2002, your $100,000 was only worth $62,385! The market had gone down for three straight years. The market had never gone down three years in a row, ever. We saw two years back-to-back during the period 1973-1974 that were negative, but not three. So, if you were wearing your big girl panties and stuck it out, by the middle of 2006 you had fully recovered and were headed into positive territory. Please know, I love my male clients BUT men are wired differently than women especially when it comes to investments. Fact is the majority of investors who bailed during these three very difficult years were men. For those of you who managed to stick it out, may I suggest you were in touch with your feminine side and were in fact wearing big girl panties…

By the end of 2007, your $100,000 investment was worth $114,062 and you were starting to feel pretty good about yourself again…until you didn't. The year erupted with the bursting of the U.S. Housing Bubble that caused the value of securities tied to real estate to plummet damaging financial institutions globally. The U.S. debt was downgraded and banks were failing left and right; conditions we had never seen before. Our $114,062 investment was worth $71,859 by the end of the year. Enough already, right?! The resiliency of the U.S. markets propelled your account value back to $104,559 by the end of 2010 and that my friend is what you call a "lost decade."

So how did all of this affect the savings account portion of the new and improved Variable Universal Life policies? Dreadfully. Bottom line, there was nowhere to hide. In fact for the first time ever, stocks and bonds lost money at the same time! Until 2008, stocks went up when bonds went down and bonds went up when stocks went down. This is the theory behind diversification. By having money invested in stocks and bonds at the same time you can effectively "smooth out" volatility. I say "theory" because it didn't work like that in 2008. Bummer!

If the stock market lost a decade, that means the savings account portion of the variable universal life policies lost a decade too. Remember, these policies are built on a term chassis. Every year the cost of insurance increases as the insured gets older. The savings account is designed to invest "the difference" of the "buy term and invest the difference" concept. In order for these types of policies to work, the savings account must grow enough to cover the higher cost of insurance in the later years of the policy OR the policyholder's premiums will increase. As you might imagine, anyone who owned variable universal life during the "lost decade" watched as the savings account portion of the policy got smaller and smaller. The cost of insurance increased and the value of the mutual funds they had the savings account invested in decreased. What a nightmare!

Let's take a moment to review. Whole life insurance is permanent insurance but the premiums are inflated to create a false "dividend" with which you can then choose to purchase more insurance. I've tried to say that a million different ways but fact is no matter how I word it, it just seems wrong. A.L. Williams came on the scene and boldly stated just that convincing thousands of whole life policy owners to trade in their policies for a new model – term life insurance. Families could now afford the coverage they actually needed and have money left over ... until the term expired leaving them with either no life insurance or higher premiums just to maintain the coverage they had. Since virtually no one invested their difference, they often could not afford to renew their term policies. What a mess! The insurance industry reacted quickly as they began to lose market share and introduced a "buy term and invest the difference" concept of their own called Universal Life Insurance. Realizing the need for affordable permanent life insurance, Universal Life combines term insurance rates with a savings account forcing the policyholder to invest the difference. This was truly revolutionary for the insurance industry but they struggled to get the savings account part right. The Universal Life policy pays a fixed rate on their savings account portion and that works great until interest rates go down. The variable life policy allows policyholders to invest their savings account portion into mutual funds and that works great until the stock market crashes. Hmmm ...what to do? What to do?

While variable universal life was still in its heydays, work began on a new concept. A concept designed around what I like to call "have your cake and eat it, too." Most of you will agree that historically investors have made more money in the stock market than they have in fixed investments like savings accounts, bonds and certificates of deposit but more money means more risks.

To combat that risk financial advisors, stock jockeys and money managers all around the world study charts and patterns in an attempt to "time" the market. You know the old adage, "buy low, sell high." Although some may be better at this than others, no one including Warren Buffet can time the market with 100% accuracy. Can you imagine what your retirement account would look like if your investments never lost money?

The single largest asset class of all but one of the largest banks in the United States is permanent cash value life insurance, commonly referred to as BOLI, or Bank Owned Life Insurance. During the recent economic crisis, banks accelerated their purchasing of BOLI as it was the single most secure investment they could make.

Wow! What do banks know that Suze Orman doesn't know?

Chapter 10 | Do You Understand Indexing?

Most of you probably have heard of a strategy called "indexing." There are index mutual funds, index ETFs (Exchange Traded Funds) and indexed universal life. Just because these three investment options sound the same does not mean they are the same. In fact, there are significant differences that you need to be aware of.

Let's begin with the definition of "index." A stock index or stock market index is a method of measuring the value of a section of the stock market. Some of the most common indexes are the Dow Jones Industrial Average (DJIA) comprised of only 30 industrial companies; the S&P 500 comprised of 500 large companies and designed to be a leading indicator of U.S. equities; and the NASDAQ composite, an index of more than 3,000 stocks that includes the world's foremost technology and biotech giants. These indexes are used as tools to describe the market and to compare the return of a specific investment to its appropriate benchmark. You may have heard someone describe a mutual fund as "beating the index". This indicates that the fund's value appreciated more than it's corresponding index over the same period of time. I might add that it is every fund manager's dream to outperform his fund's benchmark. Unfortunately, they seldom do.

I said it is every fund manager's dream to outperform his fund's benchmark. Well, that's not entirely true. An Index Fund by design attempts to mirror a specific index. The S&P 500 Index Fund owns the same stocks as the index itself, in the same proportions in an attempt to match its performance. It is worth noting here that these funds are not actively managed. There is no fund manager working to lower your risk or increase your return. The only time stocks in this fund are bought or sold is when the S&P 500 makes a change to the index itself, which is not all that often. Investors beware. These funds may be inexpensive to own, but there is absolutely nowhere to run when markets reverse, short of liquidating your position. It's worth noting here that many financial advisors, including Suze Orman, promote index funds.

This brings up another issue. Mutual funds, including index funds, are priced daily after the market closes. Note that you cannot sell a mutual fund during the day. Oh sure, you can call you financial advisor or your discount broker or even enter your order to sell online but it will not be executed until end of day. Why is that? Mutual funds are a collection of stocks and/or bonds. The value of these funds is determined once each day after all trading for the various stocks and bonds it owns has ended. So, if the market is falling sharply there is absolutely no way out until the dust has settled for that day. Yikes!

An Exchange Traded Fund (ETF) is structured much like a mutual fund in that it is a collection of stocks, bonds or commodities. The main difference is an ETF is traded like a stock. So in our example above where the market is falling sharply and you place an order to liquidate your ETF, you will receive the market price at that moment rather than the price at the end of the day. So an Index ETF owns the same positions and in the same proportions as the index it is trying to replicate BUT it is traded like a stock – immediate execution during regular trading hours. It is important to note here that both Index Funds and Index ETFs can lose money. Suze says, "ETFs are the way to go".

Based upon what we have learned thus far you might assume indexed universal life is a life insurance policy that attempts to mirror the performance of an index. On the contrary, no component of indexed universal life is invested in the stock market nor does it seek to replicate any index.

You will remember from the last chapter that universal life was a revolutionary concept for the insurance industry; combining the cost of term life insurance with a savings account in one policy was genius! They struggled however with the savings account portion. They tried paying fixed interest (fniversal life) that worked well until interest rates dropped. Then they let policyholders invest their savings portion into mutual funds variable universal life) and that worked well until the market crashed. In the late 1990s, a leader in the insurance industry introduced a version of a Universal Life Insurance policy where the savings account portion would benefit from market gains without participating in market losses. Let me say that a different way. The stock market goes up, you go up; the stock market loses 50% and the savings portion of your policy does not budge. Tell me more! Tell me more!

This new policy would allow policyholders to experience "market-like" returns without being invested in the market. I know exactly what you are thinking, "How is that even possible?" I am so glad you asked. I'd like to go back to my childhood when my mother took us shopping for school clothes. She used a service called "layaway." I bet you've used it, too. We picked out our clothes, took them to a clerk in the back of the store and paid a small fee which locked-in the price of the clothes for the next 90 days. Now, if my mother decided she did not want the clothes she was not obligated to buy them. She would simply forfeit her small layaway fee. However, if my mom came back to pick up the clothes and there had been a shortage of cotton that summer causing the price of clothes to jump by 20%, the store was obligated to sell her those clothes at the price she had locked-in 90 days before. Please make sure you understand this concept. It is key to unlocking the tremendous opportunity that is right in front of you. My mother had the "right" to buy, but was never obligated to buy. The store on the other hand was obligated to sell.

Some of you are way ahead of me but for those who aren't, the layaway transaction is known in the financial world as an option.

Now, before you start screaming about how risky options are, STOP! Do you own homeowners insurance? I'm sure you do. You pay a small fee each month, quarter or year that guarantees if your house burns down the insurance company has to build it back. My friend, you own a form of an option. So not all options are risky!

Think about this for a moment. Let's say the S&P 500 is trading today at 1,200. It's not, but it makes the math easier. What if you were able to lock-in today's price of the S&P 500 for the next 12 months? For the next year you go about your life, business as usual. Let's say at the end of 12 months, the S&P 500 has increased to 1320. All of your co-workers are whining, "wish I had invested money last year before that thing took off again". You have a grin on your face that looks like Sylvester who just swallowed Tweety Bird! Later when you get home you pull out your "layaway ticket" and run to your broker's office. You tell her you want to exercise your option to buy the S&P 500 at 1,200 and turn right around and sell it for today's going price of 1,320, realizing a $120 gain or 10%. I like it! This could work!

So what would happen if during that 12-month period the S&P 500 went down 120 points to 1,080? No big deal! It reminds me of the time we went to get our school clothes and there was a huge clearance rack at the front of the store. The clothes we had put in layaway were now marked down 20%! What would you do? You would do exactly what we did. We bought the clothes from the clearance rack instead of picking up our layaway and saved a ton of money! Remember, my mother had the right to buy but never the obligation to buy.

What we have here is a policy with term insurance costs and a savings account that is linked to the performance of an Index; thus the name, indexed universal life. The concept of linking the performance of the savings account portion of the policy to an index is nothing short of amazing! I suspect you are excited about what you have already read but there is SO much more. Because this type of policy has the potential to change your life I want to make sure you understand exactly how it works because guess what? Most financial advisors AND insurance agents do not understand how it works. Oh, they will tell you they understand how it works but they honestly don't have a clue, which is unfortunate for all parties involved.

To begin with, you have a choice. You decide whether you want a fixed strategy or an indexed strategy OR a combination of the two. If you are bearish on the stock market meaning you think it is going to go down, you can elect the fixed strategy and receive a fixed rate of interest on your cash value. As of February 2014 one company is offering 4.1% on their fixed strategy. If you believe the stock market is poised to go higher you can elect an indexed strategy that uses a formula to calculate interest credits based on the movement of a stock market index. If you have no idea which direction the market is headed you can allocate some of your cash value to each strategy. Thus far, I have only talked about the S&P 500 Index. Depending upon the insurance company, you may have others to choose from like the Dow Jones Industrial, EURO STOXX 50, Hang Seng and the Russell 2000.

To understand how the indexed strategies work, there are a handful of terms you need to become familiar with beginning with participation rate. The participation rate determines how much of the increase in the index's value applies to your policy. Let's assume the S&P 500 Index increases 10% over the next 12 months and your participation rate is 80%.

10 x 80% = 8% credited to your cash value.

If on the other hand your participation rate is 100%, you will receive a credit of 10%. Note that each insurance company will have different index strategies and different participation rates but for the most part all companies offer at least one strategy with a 100% participation rate. Frankly, it keeps things simple and I am a firm believer in keeping things simple.

With a solid understanding of participation rate, let's move on to cap rate. For those of you who already think this concept is too good to be true, the cap rate will pull things back within reach for you. If the market went up 50% in one year you would NOT receive a credit of 50% in the savings account portion of your policy. The cap rate is the maximum amount that will be credited to your cash value. Think of it as a ceiling. It "caps" the amount that is credited to your policy's cash value. Cap rates vary by strategy and may be reset at the end of the interest-crediting period (i.e. every 12 months). As of the writing of this book, several companies are offering 14% cap rates. If the index that your policy is linked to increases by 10% over the next 12 months and your participation rate is 100%, you would receive a credit of 10% not 14%. Note that you are not guaranteed a credit of 14%. You will receive a credit equal to the gain in the index your policy is linked to up to your cap rate. Why are limits placed on the amount credited to your policy? Simply put, with indexed universal life (IUL) you are giving up some of your upside potential in exchange for the downside guarantees.

It is very important that you understand the credit of 14% is NOT a 14% interest rate. It is a crediting rate that is determined by the movement of the index, your cap rate and the participation rate. BIG difference!

What are the guarantees? For starters, your cash value will never lose money because the stock market lost money. I like it! Remember our discussion earlier on Market Returns vs. Investor Returns? Once you step into a "hole" (lose money) it takes forever just to breakeven. With IUL, you no longer have to worry about stepping into any holes!

I want to go back to our discussion of the Lost Decade — the period of time between 2000 and 2010. You will recall $100,000 invested in the S&P 500 at the beginning of 2000 was worth $104,559 at the end of 2010. Below is a side-by-side comparison of $100,000 invested in the S&P 500 and $100,000 invested in an IUL policy linked to the S&P 500 Index using a 1-year point-to-point strategy with a 14% cap and 100% participation rate.

Time period	S&P 500 value	IUL value
2000	$90,890	$100,000
2001	$80,083	$100,000
2002	$62,385	$100,000
2003	$80,277	$114,000
2004	$89,011	$126,403
2005	$93,381	$132,610
2006	$108,126	$151,175
2007	$114,062	$159,474
2008	$71,859	$159,474
2009	$90,873	$181,801
2010	$104,559	$207,253

Look at what removing the downside does for your account value! Instead of $104,559 the IUL cash value grew to $207,253. Folks, that is no lost decade! Do you see what is happening here? First of all, when the market goes down for three straight years the IUL sits patiently and waits for things to turn around. Remember, IULs are NOT invested in the stock market so the value is unaffected by market losses. Once the market begins to move in a positive direction, so does the IUL but the IUL is starting from $100,000 not $62,385! Each year the growth in the IUL is locked-in and protected from potential future downturns in the index. The index in the IUL policy is also reset at the beginning of each new interest-crediting period so if the index declines you don't have to wait for the index to return to its previous level before you start participating in any future increases. This is exactly what happened in 2008 when the S&P 500 value dropped to $71,859. The IUL value locked-in and reset at $159,474. As the S&P 500 claws its way back, the IUL value soars!!!

Let's spend a moment on the worst scenario. What if the market had not turned around in the fourth year and would have gone down for 10 years in a row? Is there a minimum guarantee on IUL policies? Well the obvious minimum guarantee is 0%. And my friend, ZERO IS YOUR HERO! Who wouldn't take a "0" over losing money? No one. It's worth noting that some insurance companies offer minimum guarantees of 2 and 3%. Why would anyone go with the company offering a 2% minimum guarantee if another company offers a minimum guarantee of 3%? BE CAREFUL. Minimum guarantees cost money and will ultimately lower your cap (upside potential). If you feel you need a minimum guarantee, then you have to know how often the company evaluates the policy before you can determine which option is best for you and your family. I happen to know of a company that offers a 2% minimum guarantee that trues-up every 5 years. An example will work best here.

Year	Credit
1	3%
2	0%
3	0%
4	1%
5	4%

Over the five-year period, the policy received a total of 8% credited to the cash value. The minimum is 2% each year so that by the end of the 5th year the policy has to have received a minimum of 10% credited to the policy. In this example, the insurance company would credit an additional 2% to the cash value of the policy and the 5-year clock would start over. I also know of a company that offers a minimum guarantee of 3% but does not evaluate the policy until the policy terminates. Hmmm … . What do you think the chance of the stock market not returning an average of 3% over 20 or 30 years is? History would say chances are slim. So, on the surface the 3% minimum looks attractive when in reality the 2% minimum could add much more value to the policy. You have to ask questions people. If you don't ask, you will never know!

Is anybody getting excited? We are finally on to something here! Earlier I asked you to imagine what your retirement account would look like if your investments never lost money? With IUL, you don't have to imagine!

Unlike index funds and index ETFs, indexed universal life does not seek to replicate the performance of an index. In fact, because an investor never participates in market losses, the cash value of an IUL policy often outperforms its index making it the best choice for investors, young and old.

Chapter 11 | How Much Is Too Much?

Right now some of you are excited while others of you are standing shoulder-to-shoulder with the financial celebrities as they scream at the top of their lungs " permanent life insurance is expensive" followed by "there are better, less expensive, ways to invest your money." I think we can all agree the "better" part is now in question. I don't know about you but if I can benefit when the market goes up without losing when the market goes down, I want to know exactly how "expensive" it is compared to the alternatives.

I read an article that Forbes published in May 2013 titled, "The Heavy Toll of Investment Fees." In this article, Rick Ferri points out that investors are clearly paying too much for investment advice. He says, "The thought of giving up 40% per year in investment return to pay for portfolio management and advice would cause most people to walk away. Yet, this is the price many people pay when they hire an investment adviser to manage a mutual fund portfolio or exchange-traded fund (ETF) portfolio." In his article, Ferri uses a balanced portfolio of 60% equities and 40% bonds. Assuming equities return 7.5% and bonds return 2%, the portfolio return would be 5.3%.

$$7.5\% \times 60\% = 4.5\%$$
$$2\% \times 40\% = 0.80\%$$
$$4.5\% + 0.80\% = 5.3\%$$

Using an average expense ratio of 1.2% for equity funds and 0.9% for bonds funds, he determines that the combined expense ratio is 1.1%.

$$1.2\% \times 60\% = 0.72\%$$
$$0.9\% \times 40\% = 0.36\%$$
$$0.72\% + 0.36\% = 1.08\%$$

When you add another 1% that the typical investment advisor charges to the combined expense ratio, you are now at 2.1% in fees.

$$(2.1\% / 5.3\%) \times 100 = 39.62\%$$

Wow! Investors really are giving up 40% of their investment return! I do apologize for the math but remember I'm questioning everything now so I wanted to double-check Ferri's numbers.

Ferri believes investors should have a goal of paying no more than 15% per year in total cost. So how do you reduce your total fees by more than 60%? Ferri urges the investor to buy index funds that track the markets for a fraction of the cost.

No doubt Suze Orman would give Ferri a standing ovation as she is a big fan of ETFs and index funds. I, on the other hand, don't agree with Ferri's solution of settling for a portfolio of index funds and/or ETFs, which we know go up and down, just to save investment fees. What Ferri has done though is give us clear guidelines for judging our new found gem, indexed universal life.

Let me be clear, all life insurance policies are NOT created equal. Every insurance company is unique in their approach to policy expenses and it is not feasible for me to analyze every one of them here. Since we have found a permanent policy that offers market-like returns with guarantees, it seems logical to me to analyze a company who is a leader index universal life and has been since it was introduced in 1998.

Before we can look at expenses, we must discuss case design. First and foremost we are talking about a life insurance policy but, and a

BIG but here, we do not want to purchase any more coverage than we absolutely need in order to accomplish our goals. Note that the death benefit is a product of the amount you contribute to your policy. There is a minimum amount of insurance required in order for the IRS to approve policies as life insurance contracts and not savings accounts. Keep in mind life insurance policies are tax-free; savings accounts are not. Minimizing the death benefit keeps the cost of insurance low, allowing your cash value to accumulate faster. Secondly, I always run illustrations at a standard, non-smoker rate if in fact you do not smoke. If you are a smoker you must understand your numbers may not be as good as the ones discussed here. On the other hand, if after reviewing your labs and medical information the underwriter determines you are healthier than most men your age, your numbers may actually be better than the ones discussed here because your cost of insurance may be lower, allowing your cash value to accumulate faster. Finally, I always add a Waiver of Monthly Deductions Rider which protects the policyholder should he become totally disabled before the age of 65. This rider guarantees the policy will stay in force as long as the net cash value remains positive.

In the spirit of fairness, I have decided to analyze the expense report of three different policies for men of varying ages. If I analyze the expenses of a female's policy, the numbers will look better. Why? Because a woman's life expectancy is longer than a man's thus it is cheaper to insure a woman than it is a man of the same age. So again, if you are a woman your numbers will look better, all other things being equal.

Our first case is Mr. Gen Y, a 25-year-old, non-smoking male who wants to save $500 per month until he turns 65 years old. At age 65, he would like to be able to take annual withdrawals from his policy. The company I am using for this illustration has several indexing strategies to choose from. I have split Mr. Gen Y's cash value equally between the S&P 500 Index and the Hang Seng. The average historical return of the S&P 500 with a 13% cap and 100% participation is 8.05%. The average historical return of the

Hang Seng with a 14% cap and 100% participation is 8.4% giving us a combined rate of 8.23%. This insurance company calculates a 25-year historical average for each indexing strategy it offers. In other words, they apply the strategy's cap and participation rates to the previous 25 years to see how it would have performed in past markets which means each year the average changes because the oldest year falls off and the newest year is factored in. I am much more comfortable projecting future growth now that I know the cash value can never go down because the market goes down. Remember from Market Returns vs. Investor Returns Revealed, our retirement projections were short by 17.92% because we lost money in the stock market. By using Indexing strategies, that concern is removed.

At age 65, Mr. Gen Y's numbers are as follows:

Total premiums	$240,000
Cash value	$1,560,498
Death benefit	$1,872,598
Annual withdrawals	$194,005

I know what you're thinking. Why in the heck did we buy over $1 million worth of permanent life insurance on a 25-year-old? We didn't. The initial death benefit for Mr. Gen Y is $284,034, which is very reasonable. The reason it increased to $1,872,598 is because his cash value grew to $1,560,498. A quick calculation will show that

$$\$1,872,598 - 1,560,498 = \$312,100$$

Here's a little quiz for you. Is the cost of insurance assessed on $1,872,598 or $312,100? The naysayers would be yelling $1,872,598!! I hope you said $312,100 because that is all that is at risk for the insurance company. Are you with me? The death benefit on indexed universal life policies ALWAYS includes the cash value. So when Mr. Gen Y passes away, his beneficiary receives his death benefit of $312,100 AND his $1,560,498 of cash. Right off the bat, I think we have this five-alarm fire under control but let's keep digging. I want to know just how expensive indexed universal life really is.

How much did it cost Mr. Gen Y to generate a gain of $1,632,598 (death benefit less total premiums) over 40 years? There are several different expenses within a life insurance policy and we will go over each one in detail. For now,

Premium expense charges	$7,808
Annualized policy fee	$3,840
Policy expense charges	$5,340
Base cost of insurance	$28,568
Wellness reward amount	($2,604)
Net cost of insurance	$25,963
Rider expense charges	$24,572
Total fees (charged over 40 years)	*$67,523*

$67,523 / $1,632,598 x 100 = 4.14% over 40 years

4.14% / 40 years = 0.103% average per year

Oh, my goodness! I was not expecting to get anywhere close to the expense ratio of the Vanguard 500 Index Fund Investor Shares (0.17 as of April 28, 2014), but we did! The Vanguard 500 Index Fund is known for having the lowest fund expenses in the industry … 84% lower than the average expense ratio of funds with similar holdings. Orman and several other financial gurus recommend the Vanguard 500 Index Fund because its expenses are so low.

In the article, "The Heavy Toll of Investment Fees," Ferri also endorses index funds and believes that paying no more than 15% per year in total cost, including the adviser fee, is a good goal. Let's see how Mr. Gen Y's IUL expenses fared by Ferri's method. Remember our combined historical rate on our two indexing strategies is 8.23.

8.23 x 15% = 1.23

Since 0.103 is less than 1.23, I believe we have met Ferri's challenge! Ferri should approve of the expenses inside an indexed universal life Policy. Now, if indexed universal life is less expensive than the Vanguard 500 Index Fund, how can they say it is expensive? Maybe we are missing something. I'll keep digging.

Let's look at Mr. Gen Y's numbers at age 95 since we know the cost of insurance increases every year in an indexed universal life policy. Is this the expensive part?

Total contributions	$240,000
Net cash value	$2,808,680
Death benefit	$3,166,675
Total withdrawals	$5,820,140

If Mr. Gen Y died at age 95, he would have received $5,820,140 over 30 years (age 66 to age 95) and his beneficiary would receive an additional $3,166,675 for a total benefit of $8,986,815. How did $240,000 turn into $8,986,815? We will get to that, trust me. For now I want to focus on what it cost Mr. Gen Y to amass that much money over 70 years.

Premium expense charges	$7,808
Annualized policy fee	$6,720
Policy expense charges	$5,340
Base cost of insurance	$626,944
Wellness reward amount	($ 62,442)
Net cost of insurance	$564,501
Rider expense charges	$24,572
Total Fees	*$608,941 (charged over 70 years)*

$608,941/ $8,746,815* x 100 = 6.96% over 70 years
6.96% / 70 years = 0.099% average per year

*Total benefits less total premiums of $240,000.

Once again, we have met Ferri's challenge (0.099 is less than 1.23).

I know what you are thinking … if it sounds too good to be true, it is. Well, my daddy raised me on that notion as well but as I've gotten older I've realized it's not 100% true. I know it's hard for you to see it right now but I've done the research and these numbers are not only accurate but also completely doable. Stay with me. I promise by the end I will have answered all of your questions.

I would gladly pay $608,941 over 70 years to gain access to $8,746,815. What about you? Talk about hitting the lottery…oh yeah, did you remember that the $8,746,815 is income tax free!! We will talk more about that later. I just didn't want you to forget.

Indexed universal life prides itself on being completely transparent unlike other types of insurance policies. The expense report that accompanies a policy illustration reveals exactly where every penny of your premium goes as we've just seen with Mr. Gen Y. Now that you've seen the numbers, I want you to understand the numbers. Below are the definitions of the various expenses that Mr. Gen Y paid.

Premium expense charge is 6% of the target premium and 3% on amounts in excess of the target premium in policy years 1-10; it is reduced to 3% on all premiums in years 11+. Note that this fee is only charged when a premium is paid. In Mr. Gen Y's case, this fee stopped in year 41.

Annualized policy fee is charged monthly against the policy Account Values. This fee is currently $8/month or $96/year for the life of the policy.

Policy expense charges are charges based per $1,000 of original face amount of the illustrated policy. The Policy Expense Charge is not reduced even if the face amount is reduced at a later time. This amount is increased when the original face amount is increased.

NOTE: This charge stops at the end of year 10.

Base cost of insurance charges are based upon the insured's age, smoking status and rating class at policy issue.

Wellness reward amount is a credit applied toward the Base Cost of Insurance Charges. See below for a detailed explanation of The Wellness For Life Rider.
Net cost of insurance is the final Cost of Insurance after the Wellness Reward has been credited to the Base Cost of Insurance Charges.

Rider expense charges are based upon the insured's age, smoking status and rating class at rider issue. This charge is for the Waiver of Monthly Deductions that protects Mr. Gen Y in the event he becomes totally disabled prior to age 65. Note that this rider is not required but highly encouraged. However, if Mr. Gen Y decided not to elect this rider his expenses would be even lower!

Let's spend a few moments on the wellness reward amount. Driving safely is one way you can save money on your car insurance. What if you could save money on your life insurance by staying healthy? Well, now you can. At least one company now offers discounts to people who demonstrate they care about their health by seeing a doctor every other year.

It's that simple – you don't have to be a world-class athlete to reap the rewards. Follow these 3 easy steps to claim your rewards.

1. Schedule a physical with your doctor.
2. Ask doctor to complete and sign a qualification form.
3. Return the form.

Your premiums will NOT increase because of your doctor visit. Rewards (cost of insurance discounts) begin in policy year 3. Discounts can become more significant over time as they are multiplied by your policy's age.

Level 1 - Receive a discount on your insurance costs simply by going to the doctor for a physical.

Level 2 - Receive greater discounts on your insurance costs by going to the doctor AND maintaining your weight within a reasonable range. The "reasonable range" is unique to each insured and is printed in their policy.

We already have the cheapest rates inside of indexed universal life policies (term insurance rates) and with a little work on your part they can be even lower! I have a confession to make. I L-O-V-E, love a bargain! I bet you do, too.

Note: As of Feb. 21, 2014 the current Level 1 discount is ½% and the current Level 2 discount is ½%. However, this company will not illustrate a full 1% discount (1/2% for going to the doctor plus an additional 1/2% for staying within your recommended weight range). For illustration purposes, the company assumes you will go to the doctor. They do not assume you will stay within your recommended weight range. Why does this matter to you? It matters because if you go to the doctor AND stay within your recommended weight range your discount will be BIGGER than what I calculated in the numbers above which means your expenses would be even lower!

Now, is anyone wondering why in the world a Life Insurance Company would offer you discounts on your life insurance? I mean this stuff is supposed to be expensive, right? I read about a 41 year old male who went to his doctor to get his qualification form completed. He hadn't been feeling well so while he was there he mentioned it to his doctor. They ran a few tests and discovered that this young man actually had prostate cancer. Fortunately, it was in the very early stages and he is now cancer free. Because of the wellness rewards, this client is still alive, his quality of life is good and the insurance company did not have to pay a death benefit prematurely. Without the rider, the policyholder may not have gone to the doctor until it was too late. With the rider, everybody wins!

Before we analyze the expenses of the two other cases, you also need to know that beginning at the end of the 10th year and continuing in all subsequent years, an additional 0.60% of the average month-end Account Values for that year, is guaranteed to be credited to the policy. This statement is included in the illustration in black and white for all to see. What does that mean? Think of it like this. If your policy has a 14% cap rate, beginning in the 11th year your cap rate is 14.6%! This bonus is proprietary. Other company's policies may or may not have a similar feature.

You don't get to be the leader by doing things the way your competition does them. The company we are evaluating is an A-rated company and has been in the indexed universal life business since it came about in 1998. They believe in the power of indexed universal life and want it to be a good experience for all involved.

We have determined that the policy expenses of indexed universal life for a 25-year-old non-smoking male are more than reasonable. Let's take a look at Mr. Gen X. He is a standard, nonsmoking 45-year-old who wants to save $2,000 per month to age 65 and then begin to take annual withdrawals from his policy.

At age 65, Mr. Gen X's numbers are as follows:

Total premiums	$480,000
Cash value	$ 937,615
Death benefit	$1,446,951
Annual withdrawals	$116,395

The initial death benefit for Mr. Gen X is $509,336, which is very reasonable for a 45-year-old male. How much did it cost Mr. Gen X to generate a gain of $966,951 (death benefit less total premiums) over 20 years?

Premium expense charges	$17,271
Annualized policy fee	$ 1,920
Policy expense charges	$19,813
Base cost of insurance	$37,724
Wellness reward amount	($2,376)
Net cost of insurance	$35,348

Rider expense charges $35,922
Total fees *$110,274 (charged over 20 years)*

$110,274 / $966,951 x 100 = 11.40% over 20 years

11.40% / 20 years = 0.570% average per year

Since 0.570 is less than 1.23, I believe we have met Ferri's challenge again!

Here are Mr. Gen X's numbers at age 95. Let's see how expensive it gets as he gets older.

Total contributions $480,000
Net cash value $1,698,477
Death benefit $1,913,527
Total withdrawals $3,491,839

If Mr. Gen X died at age 95, he would have received $3,491,839 over 30 years (age 66 to age 95) and his beneficiary would receive an additional $1,913,527 for a total benefit of $5,405,366. How did $480,000 turn into $5,405,366? As I promised, we will get to that. For now let's focus on what it cost Mr. Gen X to amass that much money over 50 years.

Premium expense charges $17,271
Annualized policy fee $4,800
Policy expense charges $19,813
Base cost of insurance $401,836
Wellness reward amount ($38,788)
Net cost of insurance $363,049
Rider expense charges $35,922
Total fees *$440,855 (charged over 50 years)*

$440,855 / $4,925,366* x 100 = 8.95 % over 50 years

8.95 % / 50 years = 0.179% average per year

*Total benefits less total premiums of $480,000.

Once again, we have met Ferri's challenge (0.179 is less than 1.23). One more quick reminder; if Mr. Gen X decided not to elect the waiver of monthly deductions rider, which protects his policy in the event he becomes totally disabled before age 65, his expenses would be even lower.

I promised you three cases, so let's look at a 55 year old baby boomer. He is a standard, nonsmoking 55-year-old who wants to save $2,000 per month to age 65 and then begin annual withdrawals from his policy at age 76.

At age 75, Mr. Baby Boomer's numbers are as follows:

Total premiums	$240,000
Cash value	$513,883
Death benefit	$866,596
Annual withdrawals	$59,534

The initial death benefit for Mr. Baby Boomer is $352,713 which is actually low for a 55-year-old male. How much did it cost Mr. Baby Boomer to generate a gain of $626,596 (death benefit less total premiums) over 20 years?

Premium expense charges	$11,041
Annualized policy fee	$1,920
Policy expense charges	$20,387
Base cost of insurance	$66,461
Wellness reward amount	($4,323)
Net cost of insurance	$62,139
Rider expense charges	$21,594
Total fees	*$117,081 (charged over 20 years)*

$$\$117,081 \; / \; \$626,596 \; x \; 100 = 18.69 \; \% \; over \; 20 \; years$$

$$18.69\% \; / \; 20 \; years = 0.934\% \; average \; per \; year$$

Since 0.934 is less than 1.23, I believe we have met Ferri's challenge yet again!

Here are Mr. Baby Boomer's numbers at age 95. Let's see how expensive it gets as he gets older.

Total contributions	$240,000
Net cash value	$287,702
Death benefit	$337,751
Total withdrawals	$1,190,684

If Mr. Baby Boomer died at age 95, he would have received $1,190,684 over 20 years (age 76 to age 95) and his beneficiary would receive an additional $337,751 for a total benefit of $1,528,435. How did $240,000 turn into $1,528,435? Stay with me. We will get to it; I promise! Again, focus on what it cost Mr. Baby Boomer to amass that much money over 40 years.

Premium expense charges	$11,041
Annualized Policy Fee	$3,840
Policy Expense Charges	$20,387
Base Cost of Insurance	$174,511
Wellness Reward Amount	($ 15,128)
Net Cost of Insurance	$159,383
Rider Expense Charges	$21,594
Total fees	*$216,245 (charged over 40 years)*

$$\$216,245 \; / \; \$1,288,435^* \; x \; 100 = 16.78\% \; over \; 40 \; years$$

$$16.78\% \; / \; 40 \; years = 0.420\% \; average \; per \; year$$

*Total benefits less total premiums of $240,000.

Once again, we have met Ferri's challenge (0.420 is less than 1.23). Remember, if Mr. Baby Boomer decided not to elect the waiver of monthly deductions rider, which protects his policy in the event he becomes totally disabled before age 65, his expenses would be even lower.

I realize all of these numbers may be a bit overwhelming for some of you, so I've summarized our three cases here:

Mr. Gen Y		Mr. Gen X		Mr. Baby Boomer	
Age	Average expenses	Age	Average expenses	Age	Average expenses
65	0.103	65		0.5775	0.934
95	0.099	95		0.17995	0.420

Remember, Ferri said the average expense ratio for actively managed equity mutual funds is 1.2% and investment grade bond funds have an expense ratio of 0.9%, according to Morningstar. NOTICE: None of our cases have average expenses of 1.2%. In fact, all of our average expenses are less than the expense ratio of an investment grade bond fund except one and it's not off by much at 0.934%.

I don't know about you, but this was quite an eye-opener for me! We have discovered that indexed universal life has zero market risk, is cheaper than the average expense ratio of most mutual funds and the benefits are income tax free. Ah, yes. Let's talk about the taxes for a moment.

	Mr. Gen Y		Mr. Gen X		Mr. Baby Boomer	
Filing status	Tax bracket	Retirement income	Tax bracket	Retirement income	Tax bracket	Retirement income
IUL	0	$194,005	0	$116,395	0	$59,534
Single	28	$269,451	25	$155,193	15	$70,040
MFJ	33	$289,559	28	$161,660	25	$79,379

What I have done here is applied the retirement income from our three cases to the 2014 federal income tax brackets for both a single filer and a married filing joint (MFJ) filer. Do you realize what this means? Your stocks, bonds, mutual funds, annuities, real estate and precious metals have to outperform by 15%-33% AFTER FEES just to match the Retirement Income from the indexed universal life product. My dad used to say, "the chance of that happening is slim and slim is on his way out of town!"

$$\$269{,}451 \times 72\% \ (100\text{-}28) = \$194{,}004.72$$

Mr. Gen Y, a Single filer, earns $269,451 pays federal income tax at 28% and gets to keep $194,005. By the way, if your resident state has a State Income Tax your money has to work even harder! I should mention that some of you will also be subject to local income tax. Just remember, NONE of these 3 potential income taxes apply to income generated from an indexed universal life policy.

The notion that permanent life insurance is expensive is just not true. Some permanent life insurance may be expensive but I have clearly shown that ALL permanent life insurance policies are NOT expensive. In fact, some are quite INEXPENSIVE. Let me bring this home for you. Indexed universal life insurance isn't even close to being as expensive as all of the alternative investments the financial celebrities try and shove down your throat (i.e., mutual funds, managed money, ETFs, index funds, etc.).

Before we leave this chapter I need to address one more attack on permanent life insurance: Surrender charges. Let me help you out with this one. DON'T BUY LIFE INSURANCE UNLESS YOU ARE PREPARED TO KEEP IT! It's life insurance, for heaven's sake. Why are you worried about surrender charges? They are all waived when you die!

PART III
FINANCIAL PLANNING FOR 2015 & BEYOND

CHAPTER 12 |
Arbitrage: The 9th Wonder of the World

Albert Einstein said, "Compound interest is the eighth wonder of the world. He who understands it earns it … he who doesn't … pays it." If compound interest is the eighth wonder of the world, arbitrage must surely be the ninth!

What is arbitrage? In economics and finance, arbitrage is the practice of taking advantage of a price difference between two or more markets to capitalize on the imbalance. Have you ever known someone to finance a major purchase when they could have paid cash? If you're a savvy investor, perhaps you have purchased stocks on margin. Under what circumstances would this be considered a smart move? When money is cheap. In other words, when the interest you are paying on a loan is less than the interest you are earning on your investment, you should consider holding on to your cash and using the bank's money!

Recently, I Googled the term "Wealth accumulation." My search produced pages of results including: 3 Simple Steps to Building Wealth, Wealth Accumulation Planning, The Wealth Accumulation Stage and Wealth Accumulation and the Propensity to Plan just to name a few. There is a ton of information out there on how to accumulate wealth. It's everywhere from books to magazines, television to radio, the internet to webinars. Everywhere you turn, it seems there is a new strategy. So what? You have a bucket of money! Wouldn't you rather have a stream of cash flow?

I began to think about the baby boomers. Beginning in January

2011 and continuing for 19 years, 10,000 baby boomers turn 65 every day. This generation will inherit approximately $8.4 trillion from their grandparents and parents on top of what they have been able to save. The question is not, "How much have you accumulated?" but rather, "How do you make it last?"

Prior to 2008, 4% was widely accepted as the percentage of principal you could spend each year and remain relatively certain your money would last 30 years. After the financial crisis of 2008, that number has been reevaluated and now stands at 2.6%. Think about that for a moment. If your retirement income goal is $50,000 per year, before 2008 you needed to accumulate $1.25 million.

$$\$1,250,000 \times 4\% = \$50,000$$

If you think that is a big number you might want to brace yourself. Thanks to the financial crisis of 2008, you now need to accumulate $1,923,077. Yikes!

$$\$1,923,077 \times 2.6\% = \$50,000$$

Take a deep breath. I know this is overwhelming and right now you are thinking I don't have anything even close to that number! Stay with me. I promise I won't leave you hanging.

Let's say you are 65 years old and have been able to save $750,000 in your 401(k) or a similar retirement plan and you are ready to retire. You submit your paperwork to begin receiving $50,000 per year. I need you to stop and really think with me for the next few minutes. Don't just breeze over this information. What I am about to discuss with you is one of the key reasons people run out of money during retirement. Outside of the obvious reasons of not saving enough for retirement and living longer than expected, I believe what I am about to share with you is why even some very successful investors find themselves out of money during retirement.

How long can you expect that $750,000 to last? Simple math

would tell us that $750,000 divided by $50,000 equals 15 years. So if you retired at age 65 you would be out of money by age 80. Yikes! Not so fast you say ..."my money will still be earning interest while I take my withdrawals." Fair enough. What would you say is a reasonable rate of return to expect on your retirement assets during retirement...4%, 5%, or 6%? Since we can't afford to lose any money, we better go with 4% just to be safe! Using a simple interest calculator tells us that $750,000 growing at 4% for 30 years would be worth $2,432,600. Wow! You flew right past the $1,923,077 we discussed earlier as the amount needed to support a $50,000 annual withdrawal for life! That's awesome!! And that is where most of you would stop and celebrate. I am really sorry to rain on your parade but I simply must. I have to force you to THINK about what happens during retirement. No, I'm not talking about inflation or income taxes, but we will get to that. I'm talking about "how" you get that $50,000 out of your retirement plan(s).

Now, I know some of you are frustrated with the amount of mathematical calculations I have included in the book. So let me apologize in advance for adding yet another. Here's the problem. The majority of people walking around the planet today will believe 90% or more of everything they see, hear and read. STOP THAT! Please, stop that. You must start thinking for yourself and asking questions...and the sooner, the better! Why? Because some people are innocently spreading bad information (reciting what they have been told or overheard without researching the facts) and others flat out lie! I know those are harsh words but I will not apologize for them. You must wake up and take control of a situation that is seriously out of hand!

So, while I am on my soapbox screaming at the top of my lungs, let's do a little math together. If you take a $50,000 withdraw each year while your account receives a 4% return, your numbers will look something like this:

Year	Principal	Withdrawal	Subtotal	4% Interest	Total
1	$750,000	$50,000	$700,000	$28,000	$728,000
2	$728,000	$50,000	$678,000	$27,120	$705,120
3	$705,120	$50,000	$655,120	$26,205	$681,325
4	$681,325	$50,000	$631,325	$25,253	$656,578

Are you starting to see a pattern … more specifically, a problem? You are drawing down your savings at 6.67% (50,000 as a percentage of $750,000) and only receiving 4% return on your investment. After only four years you have spent $100,000 of your principal. It's gone folks! So the first part of the problem is that the money you are withdrawing is not being replaced which snowballs into the second part. In year 5, your $50,000 withdrawal is 7.6% of your remaining principal. Nearly double what you are projected to earn! Folks this is a recipe for disaster. You are spiraling out of control! Are you starting to see why even some very successful investors can run into trouble during retirement? And we have not even factored in inflation or taxes! Geez, Louise … .

So what's the answer? Make more, spend less or work longer. I bet that's not what you want to hear after you've worked your butt off, sacrificed and clipped coupons for the last 35 years! I mean really… how many times can you actually reuse aluminum foil? It feels like a cold slap in the face but the majority of the financial advisors today are recommending just that! Look around. Who is greeting you at the entrance to Walmart? Who is taking your order at McDonalds? It's YOU in 10,15 or 20 years unless you sit up and pay attention!! This is pure madness. Do you realize that retirees who work past regular retirement age are creating a job shortage for our college graduates? Yes! Think about it. If employees don't exit the workforce, those behind them can't move into their positions; which in turn opens up entry-level positions for our college graduates!! I dare say that is something many of you have never given any thought to. So working longer is a really bad alternative. Many of you are already living modestly and unless you take on a second job, which may be necessary for a short period of time, you have little to no say over the size of your paycheck. What to do? What to do?

Somehow we need to shift the burden of making our money last onto someone or something else. How do we do that? Take for instance the pensions of yester-year. My father worked 35+ years as a union electrician. One of the many benefits he received for the sacrifices he and his family made was a lifetime income or pension. My father very wisely elected a joint survivor payout; which allowed my mother to continue receiving his pension even after he passed. My mother doesn't have to worry about her income running out! My father shifted that burden to the pension provider years ago. As I said, these are the pensions of yester-year. They are virtually nonexistent today with the exception of government employees and a few others. We do have the annuity income riders we explored in Chapter 8 – Annuities Are Not Bad Investments. These products shift the burden of running out of money to the insurance carrier but we must remember that income is taxable. Increasing your taxable income during retirement can have negative implications. We will discuss that in a later chapter. For now, I am on a mission to discover tax-efficient income and make it last a lifetime!

I've taken Orman's quote, "We can make a difference when we think differently" to heart and I believe you should, too. Without a doubt, I am beyond ecstatic about the cost-effective benefits of indexed universal life! Certainly it requires us to open our minds and think differently about how we save for retirement. I am most intrigued by the income these products can produce. Recall Mr. Gen X from chapter 11. He contributes a total of $480,000 over 20 years. Using the IUL indexing strategy we previously discussed, it grows to $937,615 by age 65 and is projected to produce $116,395 of tax-free income from ages 66-100. Now I have to admit this completely goes against our previous 4% guideline, which was subsequently reduced to 2.6% after the financial crisis of 2008. So what gives? How can $937,615 last for 35 years when you're taking out $100,000+ per year? Looks to me like it would last 10 years at best!

Now, if you are using a highlighter, taking notes in the margin or turning down the corner of certain pages in this book…pay attention! You are about to receive the secret family recipe. C'mon. You know what I'm talking about. Your grandmother makes THE BEST pasta sauce known to man. You've tried to replicate it but you just can't seem to get it right…you're missing that secret ingredient that only grandma knows. Listen closely because the secret family recipe is about to be revealed!

The financial services industry has been trying to get it right for years but to no avail. The Insurance Industry, on the other hand, has in my opinion struck oil. What if you could receive income without having to actually withdraw it from your retirement account? What? I know that sounds kind of crazy doesn't it? But I bet 99% of you have done something just like this before! I know. I know. You think I have jumped off the deep end. Remember, we can make a difference when we think differently. Now is the time to think differently my friend. Our country is in no way shape or form adequately preparing for retirement. You have to make a change, and make it now!

For those of you who are still reading, thank you for your vote of confidence. I promised I wouldn't let you down on this one and I am a woman of my word. So, what in the world am I rambling on about? Have you ever gone to a bank and walked out with money that didn't belong to you? No. I'm not asking if you've ever robbed a bank! I'm asking if you have ever received a loan from a bank. Ah, of course you have! But what does that have to do with making my retirement income last? I'll get to that shortly. Have you ever tried to get a loan without collateral? Oh, it can be done but you must jump through several extra hoops to walk out of a bank with their money and only a promise to repay them. I think we can all agree that it is much easier to get a loan when you have assets to pledge as collateral.

Let's take this one step further. Let's say you have a child ready to go to college. They didn't receive a scholarship and don't qualify for financial aid. You are now faced with either paying cash or getting a loan. Cash is not an option but you have accumulated quite a bit of equity in your home. You could sell it and downsize, right? Yes, you could but is that really the best thing for you and your family at this point? The other option is to keep your home and borrow against your equity. So, you pledge your home as collateral and the bank provides the $50,000 to pay for college. Now, this is where it gets interesting so stay with me. Let's say your home appraised for $250,000 when you received the loan four years ago. The real estate market has appreciated quite nicely over the last 4 years. Your home is now valued at $300,000 and someone wants to buy it. Boy, that is exciting! Somebody is about to make $50,000 the question is who? Well now that seems like a silly question doesn't it? I mean you do own the home and the bank's mortgage is only $50,000. You could sell your house right now, payoff the bank and have $250,000 in your pocket which is what you had 4 years ago…I think the real estate market just funded your child's education — yah! Or, you can keep your home and capitalize on future appreciation. Does the bank care if you sell or stay? No, they don't. As long as the value of your home supports the balance on the loan they know the loan will get repaid when the property eventually sells because they have first lien.

What just happened here? The value of your asset/collateral appreciated at a higher rate than the rate on your loan. Do you remember the definition of arbitrage? Arbitrage is the practice of taking advantage of a price difference between two or more markets to capitalize on the imbalance. If you would have sold your home for $250,000, downsized and paid $50,000 cash for college what would you have? An asset valued at $200,000. By using the bank's "cheaper" money you kept your home, enjoyed a nice market value increase and now have an asset valued at net $250,000 ($300,000 less the $50,000 bank note). You, my friend, used positive arbitrage to your advantage and I bet you had never even heard of the term until you picked up this book! So how do you feel about this fancy-smancy term called arbitrage? Does it make you feel empowered? Well it should because it is about to change your life!

What if you could pledge your retirement assets as collateral and borrow your retirement income every year? Yeah, I know ... I'm dreaming. Think about it though. Instead of withdrawing part of your principal each year, ALL of your money would continue to benefit from interest credits. Let's go back to our earlier example and apply this "new" way of thinking.

Year	Principal	4% interest	Total	Loan	Net
1	$750,000	$30,000	$780,000	$50,000	$730,000
2	$780,000	$31,200	$811,200	$100,000	$711,200
3	$811,200	$32,448	$843,648	$150,000	$693,648
4	$843,648	$33,746	$877,394	$200,000	$677,394

Compared to the "old" way of slowly liquidating your retirement assets:

Year	Principal	Withdrawal	Subtotal	4% interest	Total
1	$750,000	$50,000	700,000	28,000	728,00
2	$728,000	$50,000	678,000	27,120	705,120
3	$705,120	$50,000	655,120	26,205	681,325
4	$681,325	$50,000	631,325	25,253	656,578

The gain over four years is $20,816. We are moving in the right direction!!

Guess what? I'm not dreaming. This is EXACTLY what the Insurance Industry figured out and the Financial Services Industry doesn't want you to know! Now for all you naysayers out there, yes "interest" accrues on the outstanding loan balance. Let's go ahead and address that right now. What you think is a negative is actually quite positive!

Earlier when you got a loan from the bank to pay for your child's college education, did you report that as income on your tax return the following year? That's absurd! Of course not! You don't report loan proceeds as income. Why not? Simple. Loan proceeds have to be repaid. Hmmmm...this is starting to get very interesting. Do you report income from retirement accounts on your tax return? With the exception of income from a Roth IRA you betcha you do! Whoa...wait a minute. Have we discovered a loophole? Am I saying that if people ... YOU ... use an indexed universal life policy as your vehicle of choice to fund your retirement and then "borrow" your income instead of actually withdrawing it, you can avoid paying income tax? Oh, my, ... I think that IS what I am saying!

This is a whole new ballgame people! We have to reevaluate the numbers. Assuming your effective income tax rate is 20%, when you withdraw $50,000 from your retirement assets you only get to keep $40,000. Sorry, not my rule. If you wanted to receive $40,000 from your indexed universal life policy you would borrow ... $40,000.

Year	Principal	4% interest	Total	Loan	Net
1	$750,000	$30,000	$780,000	$40,000	$740,000
2	$780,000	$31,200	$811,200	$80,000	$731,200
3	$811,200	$32,448	$843,648	$120,000	$723,648
4	$843,648	$33,746	$877,394	$160,000	$717,394

After four years of borrowing $50,000, our net account value from above was $677,394. We now have $40,000 MORE because we had to borrow less. Do you realize that in this example pledging your retirement assets as collateral and borrowing your retirement income just added another year to the life of your asset? Are you starting to see how Mr. Gen X can have just shy of $1,000,000 at retirement, borrow $100,000 per year and not run out of money? Is this exciting or what?

Ok, if this is so easy why is everyone not doing it? Let's face it; we have heard our entire lives to max out your 401(k), grab the "free money," i.e., company match and pay lower taxes in retirement because you will make less money then. Hopefully by now you realize these are all set up to encourage you to play the retiree game hosted by none other than Uncle Sam himself!

Arbitrage is not foolproof. You can experience negative arbitrage if you are not paying attention. Negative arbitrage is when it actually costs you more to borrow money than your collateral is earning; you are losing money, not making money.

As I researched this new way of thinking, I discovered there are different types of loans that can assist in managing the risk of negative arbitrage: variable and fixed. The first is exactly what it sounds like and the most popular. The rate can change during the life of the loan. That's not unusual. Many of us have adjustable rate mortgages or lines of credit whose rates are tied to the prime rate. As the prime rate goes up and down, so does the rate on the debt. Without going into a great amount of detail here (this is something you should work with an agent on), an illustration can say just about anything the agent wants it to say, so be careful.

Most of the insurance carriers do place limitations on how much income an agent can illustrate to the client, but some of these carriers' guidelines are quite generous. For example, let's look at an 8% historical crediting rate with a 4% loan rate. The illustration projects the future values of your cash based upon a 4% spread (8%-4%). This is way too aggressive. Research has shown that the probability of a spread this large existing over a period of 30 years is zip and zero! There is, however, a 90% chance that a 1% spread could exist for the duration of your retirement. Personally, I like to use a 2% spread when I run illustrations. There is a high probability that these conditions will exist, and in years where negative arbitrage might rear its ugly head, I have the option of switching to a fixed loan.

A fixed loan is basically a "wash" loan. This means if your interest credit for the year is 6%, your loan will accrue 6% interest for that year effectively "washing out" your gain. It is interesting to note here that most carriers allow you to switch from variable to fixed and back again multiple times during the life of the loan. In my opinion, these loan features make this new way of thinking look even better!

Now before we leave this subject, I need to speak to the naysayers one more time. We might actually get them to agree that using an indexed universal life policy as the vehicle to fund your retirement can cost-effectively produce tax-free income for life but they will follow that up with something like, "and once the government figures out what is going on they will close that loophole faster than you can say, 'Sha-zam!' " Well, the government might want to close that loophole but they can't. How can I be so sure? An indexed universal life policy is a contract. Per the constitution of the United States, contracts cannot be changed once issued. 401(k) guidelines, however, are laws taken directly from the tax code. Last time I checked laws can be and are changed on a regular basis.

So there you have it … arbitrage, the secret ingredient! Is it possible that we might actually have a solution to the retirement problem in America?

Chapter 13: The Domino Effect

Did you play with dominos when you were a child? I was never interested in the mathematical game of dominos. I was more interested in standing hundreds, sometimes thousands of those little guys on their end just so I could watch them fall. Sounds crazy, I know. Some of you reading this book know exactly what I'm talking about because you did it, too. If you were patient and had the time, you could create some beautiful displays. Watching the effects of just ONE domino unfold could be a masterpiece. But at times it could be so frustrating! You would be hours into your project only to bump the table … ahhhhhh. Sometimes you could stop the chain of events before it destroyed your entire work of art. Other times, you stood there and watched as your entire project came crashing down. What did you do? You started over and this time you moved more strategically, using great care to protect your masterpiece.

I can't help but think of retirement when I talk about dominos. I mean think about it. There is so much to consider and more times than not, one decision can impact so many others. Oftentimes, people leave too much space in between their "retirement dominos" and everything comes to a screeching halt. Other times, they didn't take the time to put enough "retirement dominos" on the table; their masterpiece is beautiful albeit short-lived. This chapter discusses various aspects of retirement that if properly orchestrated can make your golden years much less stressful and far more enjoyable.

There are many things to think about as you begin to prepare for retirement. As with any major project, the sooner you start the better prepared you will be. When I talk with clients about their impending retirements the conversation often circles around Social Security, IRAs, and pensions for the few who will actually receive one. Don't get me wrong, these are very important subjects but there is so much more. I get the biggest kick out of hearing a financial advisor ask her client how much income he wants or will need during retirement. How do you answer that? Some advisors take it a step further and ask, "How much income would you like in today's dollars?" They at least acknowledge the fact that inflation is real. We will get to that shortly. For now, let's talk more about how much income you will need during retirement.

When I work with clients, I approach this subject a little differently. What if you retired at age 65 with $1 million, decided to live modestly on $50,000 per year, only to die at age 75? Your decision to live on $50,000 per year was so that your money would last a lifetime, right? Of course! If you knew you only had 10 years to live you could have taken $100,000 per year and really enjoyed the time you had left. The problem is we don't know when we are going to die. Well, we might not know the exact date and time, but there are tools available these days that can provide a high probability as to when it may occur. Now, I know I just completely tripped you out and you probably don't want to read any further, but you simply must keep reading.

You can't properly save for something if you don't have a relatively good idea how much it is going to cost. If you need a new car and have a $25,000 budget, chances are you are not going to waste your time looking at new BMWs. I have a friend who loves to window shop. Her husband can't stand it and often refuses to go with her. Women often get labeled as "shoppers" and I don't think that is necessarily a bad thing. Window-shopping is like doing research.

Once we know what we want and how much it costs, we can begin saving toward our goal.

Retirement is no different. It pains me to see advisors cranking out cookie-cutter retirement plans with income between ages 65-95. Why 30 years? Because that is what they have been trained to do. It's as simple as that. The larger companies believe that if they project 30 years of income, somehow they are less likely to be held responsible if in fact you do run out of money. They will use the excuse you lived longer than they anticipated. But did they take any measures to even determine how long that might actually be? I doubt it. In fact, I have come across very few advisors who incorporate this step into their process. That doesn't change the fact that it is a very useful tool in helping you plan for the best retirement possible.

The tool is called a Longevity Report. It's one of the coolest things I have come across in my entire career. As soon as I discovered it, I did one on myself. I found out that I have a 10% chance of living to be 101 years of age. So what exactly is a Longevity Report? It's a report that tells you when you are going to die. Well, not exactly. But it is a report that will tell you the probability of when you are going to die. I realize that is not something we like to dwell on but when you are planning for retirement knowing how long you need to plan for is an important part of the equation.

Ladies, you should know that we are expected to live five years longer than men. In fact, 85% of people over the age of 100 are women! Men insert joke here_____.

C'mon, you have to agree that's pretty neat! Honestly, I can't believe the financial services industry hasn't picked this up and run with it before now. Insurance companies do it every day. You apply for life insurance. They look at your age, sex, whether or not you smoke, the answers to a few medical questions, then determine the probability of when you are statistically "supposed" to die and charge you a premium accordingly. Incorporating a Longevity Report into your financial plan should be a no-brainer!

So, we get your report and it says you have a 10% chance of living to age 75. Well that kind of stinks, BUT now I can comfortably advise you to take more income and enjoy the time you have left. Sounds good, right? Not so fast you say. I know what you're thinking: "So what happens if I DO live to be 75 or 80 or even 85? If I take more money in the first 10 years I will be broke if I beat the odds." Not if I designed your retirement plan. You always have to have a Plan B. That's just good business.

In chapter 9, we learned about term life insurance. The death benefit is only paid if you die before the term ends. What if there was a product that only paid if you were still ALIVE at a certain age? Would that make you feel better about taking more money in the first 10 years? Well, it should! I call this product "Longevity Insurance." At retirement, I carve out a small lump sum of money to purchase a policy that would continue your monthly income for life should you live beyond age 75. Oh, and just so you know, I always add a return of premium rider to that policy, which means if you don't beat the odds and in fact do pass before age 76, the lump sum of money we used to purchase the longevity insurance is returned to your estate. No harm, no foul!

You have to admit using longevity Iinsurance in conjunction with a Longevity Report gives your financial plan a solid foundation. No more guessing. No more cookie-cutter income projections from age 65-95. This is your retirement! If you don't get it right, there are no do-overs!!

Now that we have realistic expectations for how long you are expected to live, the next question is "what will your quality of life be during retirement?" I know these things aren't fun to talk about but they must be addressed if you plan to enjoy your retirement. Circumstances can change in a blink of an eye. You could be in an accident, paralyzed from the neck down. You could develop Alzheimer's disease. You could have a stroke and live. These are all frightening situations to be in and quite expensive, I might add. Ignoring the possibility that it could happen does not mean it won't happen. So, we plan for the worst and hope for the best!

What exactly is long-term care? Long-term care refers to a continuum of medical and social services designed to support the needs of people living with chronic health problems that affect their ability to perform everyday activities. In fact, most long-term care insurance requires that you NOT be able to perform two of the six ADLs (activities of daily living) before you can begin to receive your benefits. ADLs include eating, bathing, dressing, toileting, transferring (walking) and continence.

So who will need long-term care? According to www. LongTermCare.gov nearly 70% of people turning age 65 can expect to use some form of long-term care during their lives. That means you. Yes, you! I don't care if you are reading this book and only 45 years old. Long-term care is a real risk for you, even more so than others as the costs are only going to rise over time. Once you understand you have risk, the smartest move you can make is deciding how you will handle it. The average length of stay in a nursing home is 3.7 years for a woman and 2.2 years for a man. Now we can begin to get an idea of the potential liability you might have ahead. The cost of care will differ by state and region. Since I am a resident of Florida and we have quite a large population of seniors, I have decided to highlight Florida's 2014 Annual Care Costs. If you live in a different state, go to https://www.genworth. com/corporate/about-genworth/industry-expertise/cost-of-care. html for your local rates. Please understand I am not endorsing Genworth or any of their products. I did, however, find their sight to be the easiest to use and the most up to date.

Home Care Annual Cost	5-Yr Annual	Growth
Homemaker services	$40,612	1%
Home health aide	$42,328	1%
Adult day health care	$15,600	2%
Assisted living facility		
Private, one bedroom	$36,000	5%
Nursing home		
Semi-private room	$83,950	4%
Private room	$91,615	4%

To properly prepare, you need to understand the various types of care available. First there is home care, which consists of homemaker services and home health aides. Homemaker services are exactly what they sound like. These services allow you to stay in your home or return to your home by helping you complete regular household task that you can't manage alone. These services include cleaning house, cooking meals and running errands. The cost seen in the chart is based upon 44 hours per week for 52 weeks. Home health aides offer more extensive care to people who need more personal care than family and friends are able or have the time to provide. Again, the cost is based upon 44 hours per week for 52 weeks.

Adult day health care provides service at a community-based center for adults who need assistance or supervision during the day but do not need round-the-clock care. The centers may provide health services, therapeutic services and social activities. The number in the chart represents the cost for five days per week for 52 weeks.

Assisted living facilities are arrangements that provide personal care and health services for people who may need assistance with activities of daily living (ADLs), but who wish to live as independently as possible and who do not need the level of care provided by a nursing home. It's important to note that assisted living is not an alternative to a nursing home, but an intermediate level of long-term care.

Nursing home care is for people who may need a higher level of supervision and care than in an assisted living facility. They offer residents personal care, room and board, supervision, medication, therapies and rehabilitation, as well as skilled nursing care 24 hours a day.

Are you paying attention? Depending upon the level of care you may need, the annual costs range from $15,600 to almost $92,000 per year. Great day in the morning! How many of you are expecting to have after-tax retirement income of $92,000 per year? Probably not many AND if you do, it could take every dime of it just to take care of you or your spouse should you need long-term care…let's hope and pray you BOTH don't need it. Keep in mind if you are one of the lucky few who can afford $92,000 per year to care for your spouse in a nursing home, will there be enough income left over to support you?

I believe I heard one of you say something about Medicare … something to the effect of "doesn't Medicare cover long-term care"? Uhhh … NO! Medicare does not pay for long-term care needs. According to www.longtermcare.gov, Medicare does not pay the largest part of long-term care services or personal care — such as help with bathing, or for supervision often called custodial care. Medicare will help pay for a short stay in a skilled nursing facility, for hospice care, or for home health care if you meet the following conditions:

• You have had a recent prior hospital stay of at least three days.

• You are admitted to a Medicare-certified nursing facility within 30 days of your prior hospital stay.

• You need skilled care, such as skilled nursing services, physical therapy, or other types of therapy.

If you meet all these conditions, Medicare will pay for some of your costs for up to 100 days. For the first 20 days, Medicare pays 100 percent of your costs. For days 21 through 100, you pay your own expenses up to $152 per day ($157.50 in 2015), and Medicare pays any balance. You pay 100% of costs for each day you stay in a skilled nursing facility after day 100. Yikes! The average stay for a woman is 3.7 years. That's 1,351 days. So unless you plan to die on day 101, you will be 100% financially responsible for 1,250 more days. Talk about a financial nightmare! I think we can agree Medicare is not the answer.

Now that I have your attention, you have probably begun to think about traditional long-term care insurance. STOP! Stop right where you are! The answer is NOT in traditional long-term care insurance either. Sorry to cut you off but there's absolutely no point in wasting your time. You should know that I used to sell traditional long-term care insurance and thought I was doing a bang-up job for my clients. Then I fired the "salesperson" in me and began to analyze the policies. First of all, unless you have a "return of premium" rider on your policy you will receive NO benefits unless you qualify by not being able to complete 2 of the six ADLs (eating, bathing, dressing, toileting, transferring/walking and continence). Now I know that sounds kind of silly but this stuff is NOT cheap. So, to pay for something that you may never use is concerning to me. If you think you are going to protect yourself by adding the "return of premium" rider, please think twice. Although this option is certainly better than having the coverage without the rider, it is MORE expensive. In essence you would be tying up a substantial amount of money for what? The warm fuzzy feeling you get inside by knowing if anything were to happen you would be covered? C'mon! That's not a good reason to make a bad choice! Let's say you do qualify for benefits only to find out your policy does not cover home health services. What!? You would much rather stay in the comfort of your own home but you've paid for coverage and the only way to receive benefits is by moving into an approved nursing facility. Yuck! Although most of today's policies do provide benefits for home health services, for the most part traditional long-term care insurance is expensive and way too restrictive.

What else is there? I'm glad you asked. Today's retiree who can make a difference by thinking differently, must make his dollars stretch as far as possible. For some of you this will come quite easily…for others, not so much. I was raised to never pay full price for anything. It had to be on sale, I had to use a coupon or better yet it was on sale, I had a coupon AND the store was doubling coupons that week! When you don't have much, you learn how to stretch every dollar you get. With that in mind, we need to focus on retirement products that stretch our dollars … the industry calls this leverage.

Hold that thought for a moment and let's talk about inflation, another serious threat to your retirement. So how much was gas when you were a kid? What about a postage stamp, the price of a new car or a new house? I love the website http://www.dmarie.

com/timecap. If you go there and type in your birthdate, you can find out what everything costs on the day you were born. The day I was born, gas was $0.32 per gallon, a postage stamp was $0.05, a new car was $2,410, a new house was $23,300 and the Dow Jones Industrial Average was 786. In comparison, today gas is $3.23/gal where I live ... even higher in some parts of the country. A postage stamp costs $0.49 each. The average price of a new car is $31,252. The average price of a new home is $320,100. And, the Dow Jones Industrial Average closed at 17,042.90. Is any of this starting to sink in? The price of a postage stamp doubled 3.23 times over 48 years. If that happens over the next 48 years, the cost of a first-class postage stamp will climb to $4.82 each! A gallon of gas doubled 3.26 times over 48 years. At that rate, when I am 96 years old, a gallon of gas will cost $32.56 a gallon. Now, I know what you are thinking: "There is no way a gallon of gas will cost $32.56 48 years from now!" Hmmm ... in 1966 if you had said, "there is no way a gallon of gas will cost $3.23 in 48 years," I bet my mom would have agreed with you. BUT HERE WE ARE. Folks, inflation is real and it is one of the BIGGEST threats to your successful retirement.

The long-term average for inflation is 3.33% annually. As of August 2014, the U.S. inflation rate is at 1.70%, compared to 1.99% last month and 1.52% last year. The pattern that is starting to develop supports my concern that inflation could be poised to rear its head in a very ugly way sooner than later. Over the past couple of years, inflation has been extremely low. My fear is that we have become complacent. If your financial advisor is not discussing inflation with you, you need a new advisor.

Let's look at a quick scenario. Say you are 20 years away from retirement with an income goal of $50,000 per year. If inflation averages just 1% over the next 20 years, you will need $61,009.50 to maintain your purchasing power. If inflation averages 2%, you will need $74,297.37 and God forbid it reach 3%! To retire in 20 years with $50,000 in today's dollars adjusted for 3% inflation means you would need $90,305.56. Can you imagine getting to your retirement party and instead of having $50,000 a year to live on you only had $25,000? Folks, you better take note because that is EXACTLY what is going to happen if you are not factoring inflation into your retirement plan. And, the longer you have until retirement the worse this problem gets!

We can't have a conversation about retirement planning without discussing taxes. Before we get started, you should know that I am not going to be siding with any political party's agenda. What I am going to do though is take what I believe to be a very realistic approach to the topic of "Retirement Planning For 2015 And Beyond." So, here's the $64,000 question: Do you think taxes will go up or go down in the future? Unfortunately, my crystal ball broke last week — dang it — so I don't have the answer BUT I believe I can make an educated guess.

Go back with me to your first full-time job. Do you remember listening to the HR manager tell you about the various benefits that came along with your job? There was medical and dental insurance, vision and prescription drug coverage, supplemental life insurance, disability and a retirement plan. Do you remember why she told you it would be a good idea for you to participate in this plan? I would bet a hundred dollar bill she said something like, "you won't pay tax on the money you contribute to the plan until you withdraw it later in retirement and since you will be making less money in retirement than you are today, you will be in a lower tax bracket so you will actually save money by participating in this plan … AND for every dollar you save, the company will match it with 0.25 up to 3%." Am I right? So, you talked to a couple guys in the break room that afternoon and decided it was a good idea.

For others of you, that advice may have come from a CPA. You may be a small business owner looking for every tax deduction you can possibly find. Why? I do not know but we will get to that shortly. You may have opened a SIMPLE Plan, a SEP or maybe some of you established a solo 401(k). What is pushing you to do this? It's like everything these days … you want it now. From the microwave to credit cards we can't seem to wait for anything anymore. You want the most money you can possibly have TODAY and you will sell your soul to the devil to get it. Bad move, dude. Your dominos are going to tumble faster than you ever thought possible!

Our national debt currently stands at $17,781,487,901,300.17 and grows daily. According to www.davemanuel.com/us-national-debt-clock.php every man, woman and child in the United States currently owes $58,525 for their share of the U.S. public debt. I hate to ask, but where is that money going to come from? Even if the government proposed, passed and lived by a balanced budget starting tomorrow WE STILL OWE $17,781,487,901,300.17!! You can't just ignore nearly18 trillion dollars!

If I were to ask 100 people walking down the sidewalk today if they thought their taxes were high or low, the better majority of them would reply, "High." The Center on Budget and Policy Priorities disagrees. They reported on April 15, 2014, that Federal taxes on middle-income Americans are near historic lows. Stating further that federal income taxes on middle-income families have declined significantly in recent decades. Folks, please don't be sucked into some politician's campaign that he or she is going to lower your taxes once elected. It is not mathematically possible.

Nearly every person I work with tells me their main objective in retirement is to maintain their lifestyle. That's great. I have the same objective. So now think with me for a moment. If things are going to cost more because of inflation and tax rates are expected to climb, are you going to need more or less money in retirement? Is the light bulb starting to flicker yet? You will need MORE money in retirement than when you were working just to maintain your lifestyle. You say, "but my house will be paid off." Ok fine, so your house will be paid off but now your health-insurance costs have gone through the roof and you want to travel. Unless you suffer a devastating financial crisis at or near retirement, your taxes will NOT be lower in retirement than they are today.

That brings me to Social Security. No doubt the program needs an overhaul but I am here to tell you, it is not going away. How do I know that? Because as of August 2014, there were 63,808,000 people receiving some form of Social Security benefit, and 42,557,000 of which were age 65 or older. So what do you think would happen if all of the sudden nearly 64 million people stopped receiving their monthly benefits? A revolution is what would happen. So although there may be changes to the program, I have every confidence in the world that Social Security will be around when you go to retire.

So when is the best time to begin receiving benefits? All of you at once said: "as soon as we can get them!" Not so fast. Social Security can play a big role in your retirement. Strategically planning when you receive your benefits may go a long way in reducing your overall income taxes during retirement. Let me say that again. Strategically planning when you receive your benefits may go a long way in reducing your overall income taxes during retirement. Do you realize that if you reach your retirement goal of maintaining your lifestyle there is a strong possibility you will pay income tax on 85% of your social security benefits? I said that to a client recently and he squinted his eyes and said, "you mean I'm going to pay tax on a tax?" Yes, you may pay tax on a tax unless you put things in place now to reduce or possibly avoid it.

Here's the deal. If you are single and have less than $25,000 (married and have less than $32,000) in combined income, you have absolutely nothing to worry about. What is "combined income"? The IRS defines combined income as your adjusted gross income plus any tax-exempt interest — which could be interest from municipal bonds and savings bonds — plus 50 percent of your Social Security benefits.

If you are single and have combined income between $25,000 and $34,000 (married and have combined income between $32,000 and $44,000), 50% of your Social Security benefits may be taxed as ordinary income. What exactly does that mean? If you make $22,000 a year, are in the 20% tax bracket and receive $20,000 in Social Security benefits, you may owe the government $2,000 income tax on your Social Security benefits alone.

$22,000 + (\$20,000 \times 50\%) = \$32,000$ combined income

50% of Social Security is taxed as ordinary income.

$20,000 \times 50\% = \$10,000 \times 20\% = \$2,000$

Now, if you are single and have more than $34,000 a year combined income ($44,000 a year combined income if you are married), 85% of your benefits will be taxed as ordinary income. Geez Louise! You now owe $3,400 income tax on your Social Security benefits.

$20,000 \times 85\% = \$17,000 \times 20\% = \$3,400$

Remember, if that $44,000 happens to come from tax-free municipal bonds...you will still owe $3,400 income tax on your Social Security benefits. The definition of "combined income" includes tax-exempt interest from municipal bonds and savings bonds. Sorry!

So, how do you avoid paying tax on a tax? A couple of things come to mind. The first would be to keep your combined income under the $25,000 and $34,000 limits. Sounds easy enough, right? Well, I think it's safe to say if you do that you won't be maintaining your current lifestyle, which means your retirement will be stressful. Doesn't sound like a very good option now that I think about it. Another idea is to strategically plan the timing of your benefits. Currently, for every year you delay your benefits, they increase by 8% to age 70 — not a bad deal. Is it feasible to draw down taxable assets before you receive your social security benefits? Perhaps.

CNN Money reports that, "Only one savings plan gives you the chance to free yourself from taxes in retirement". The article goes on to say, "withdrawals from ROTHs are excluded from this calculation (combined income). So by pulling money from a ROTH account instead of other sources, you may be able to protect some or all of your Social Security check from the IRS, thus boosting your after-tax income in a given year". Although I agree with CNN Money that Roth IRAs have the ability to boost your after-tax income, I am going to have to disagree with them that "only one savings plan gives you the chance to free yourself from taxes in retirement.

Do you remember me asking in chapter 12 if you report loan proceeds as income on your tax return? I know. I know. That is a ridiculous question. You do NOT report loan proceeds on your income tax return. Loan proceeds are not considered income because they have to be repaid. What does any of this have to do with anything? You will recall that indexed universal life allows you to pledge your account value as collateral and begin receiving income in the form of "loans." Do you see where I am going with this? Instead of funding an IRA, a 401(k) or any other type of tax-deferred vehicle, what if you actually used an IUL policy as your retirement vehicle? By accessing your cash value via loans, you would receive all of your income tax-free including your social security benefits. Wow! Although I have affectionately referred to IUL plans as Roth IRAs on steroids, in the next chapter we will discuss some key differences between a Roth IRA and an IUL that just may have you rearranging your retirement dominos.

Before we leave this chapter, we need to spend a few moments on pensions. I realize pensions are nearly a thing of the past but there are still a handful of folks, some reading this book, who will be eligible for a pension whether it be from the government or the private sector. Pensions are also known as defined benefit plans. They are funded by your employer and do exactly what their name implies: provide a monthly benefit for life. Every plan is a little different. I can't possibly cover every option but I do want to hit some highlights of the most common plans. If you are eligible for a pension at retirement, please do not make a hasty decision about how you will receive your benefits. Consider your options and select the best choice for you and your loved ones.

One of the most common ways to receive your benefits is lifetime income. I'll admit that sounds pretty good on the surface. On your last day of work you stroll into the HR department to discuss how you would like to receive your retirement benefits. The HR manager explains you are eligible to receive a lifetime benefit of $2,500 per month. You think about that for a moment. Your house is paid for, your car is paid for, you have no credit card debt, and you think, I can manage pretty well on $2,500. For those of you who are married, can you tell me what happens when that retiree dies? Does the income continue to the spouse? Is the amount reduced? Answer: If the retiree elected a life annuity the income stops at the death of the recipient. Bottom line, there is no "life" in which to base the benefits on. Yikes! You could retire today, elect a life annuity, get run over by a semi tomorrow and the company would get to keep ALL of the money they had set aside for your benefit. All of the sudden what you thought was a pretty good idea just left a really bad taste in your mouth. Now, some of you aren't as put off by that idea because you aren't married. But wouldn't it be nice if someone you actually cared about got some of that money when you died instead of the company getting to keep it all? I'd like to think the answer to that question is, "yes."

There are a couple of ways you can make sure the scenario in the last paragraph does not happen to you and the people you care about. First, some pension plans actually give you an option to take a lump-sum distribution. Ahhhh … that's interesting! Let's take a minute and think about what happens to the money that the company has set aside for you when you retire. If you elect a life annuity, the company actually purchases an annuity contract on your life from an insurance company. Why do they do that? It's called shifting the risk. Frankly, the company does not want the liability of having to pay you a check every month until you die. What if they invest the money poorly? What if you live to age 121? How will they continue to pay your monthly income? Rather than deal with any of that, it's much easier for them to purchase an annuity on your behalf. This way they know your benefits will be paid each and every month. Have you ever thought if they can do that why can't I? If your pension plan offers a lump-sum distribution option, you can! By electing this option, you maintain control of your asset. I'm thinking with the amount of corruption we have seen in the financial sector, this may be appealing to some of you. When you take a lump-sum distribution and reinvest it you have control over what happens to any remaining balances when you die whether that is tomorrow or in 30 years. Pretty neat! By the way, there is absolutely no reason the retiree can't purchase his own annuity with a guaranteed income rider and death benefit insuring that he will receive a check every month AND any remaining balance at his death would go to his designated beneficiaries. If your pension plan offers a lump-sum distribution option, I would give it serious consideration.

Now, for those of you who do not have a lump-sum distribution option, there are still a couple of ways to protect yourself. One way is to elect a joint-survivor annuity. This means that your spouse would continue to receive benefits after you die. This also means that you won't receive $2,500 per month. Instead, you receive a smaller amount effectively creating a savings account for your spouse that she can draw against when you die. This option deserves a closer look. To begin with, wouldn't a customized longevity planning report come in handy here! Lifetime income is a crapshoot. You are hoping to live to age 100 and the annuity company hopes you die the day after you retire! It's true!! So having a handle on your life expectancy would certainly put you at an advantage in selecting the best pension option. Let's say they offer you a 50% joint annuity that pays $2,000 per month. You give up $500 per month so that your spouse can receive $1,000 per month when you die. Is that a good deal? I don't know! If you were my client and insurable, I would run a life insurance quote for $300,000 on your life and see if it costs more than $500 per month. Why $300,000? When you die, your spouse would receive $300,000. Reinvested at a conservative rate of 4%, that will produce $12,000 per year or $1,000 per month. Now, what if $300,000 of permanent life insurance is LESS than $500 per month? What if it only costs

$400 per month? Wouldn't that be neat? You could comfortably take the life annuity for $2,500 per month, purchase $300,000 of permanent life insurance for $400 per month netting $2,100 per month. You receive more income from your pension and your spouse is protected when you die. See? You can't just make a quick decision on pension payouts. There is a lot to consider.

Finally, for those of you who may be eligible for a pension and are not married, my social security number is … oh, sorry! Seriously though, if you died prematurely wouldn't you want your retirement benefits to go to someone you cared about instead of back to the company? I'm thinking you would. You can guarantee that someone will receive benefits for a certain period of time by electing the "period-certain" pension option. There may be a 10-year period certain, a 15-year period certain or maybe even a 20-year period certain. Understand, the longer you guarantee your benefits the lower the benefit amount goes. Also understand that when you elect this option you will receive your benefits until the day you die even if you live to be age 121. What you are guarding against is a premature death. So, if you elected 20-year period certain and died 10-years into your retirement your designated beneficiary would continue to receive your pension benefits for 10 more years. Likewise, if you elected the 10-year period certain option and died 10-years into your retirement your benefits would stop. In this latter option the insurance company's liability was for 10 years and they met their liability.

As you can see, pensions deserve a little more thought than an exit interview with your HR manager. I highly recommend you begin your discussion at least 90 days prior to retirement. This gives you ample time to discuss the information with your family and your financial advisor. In addition, if you are considering taking a life annuity and purchasing a life insurance policy with a portion of the benefits that policy needs to be approved and issued PRIOR to electing your life annuity benefit. Pension elections are irrevocable. If you choose the life annuity then decide to purchase a life insurance policy only to find out you are uninsurable, you

CANNOT go back and switch to a 50% joint-survivor annuity.

In this chapter we have discussed life expectancy, longevity insurance, long-term care, inflation, taxes, Social Security and pensions. As I've written this chapter, it didn't occur to me until now that most of these areas are pretty much out of our control. With the exception of life expectancy and long-termcare, your retirement is at the mercy of the law. Laws can and do change every day altering our domino sequence. It makes sense then to control what you can. This may seem obvious but I talk to people every day who are blindly walking into their future believing everything they see, hear and read. Please stop! Solutions must be assessed, not blindly accepted!

Chapter 14 | Your Future Self

As a child, we were all asked, "What do you want to be when you grow up?" Some of you said a doctor maybe even a lawyer, while others said a fireman or policeman, maybe even the president of the United States. My point is that it is completely normal for a child to think about what he wants to be when he grows up. How many of you have stopped to think about who you will be in retirement … your Future Self? Will you volunteer? Will you teach a yoga class? Will you travel? Use the space below to write down a description of who you want to be and what you want to do when you get to retirement age. Go ahead. Please. Do it right now.

_____

_____

_____

For me, retirement means I no longer have to work. I may choose to work because I absolutely love helping people but I will not have to work in order to financially support myself. I want to use some of my time to travel, but I also want to stop and take time to give back; to volunteer, whether it be serving in the soup kitchen, walking dogs at the local humane society or reading to school children. This part-time, traveling volunteer is a real person. She is my Future Self. As such it is my responsibility to take care of her, to provide for her. Seems odd. I know. How do you take care of something that doesn't exist? Well it's not easy and most of us fight it daily. Art Markman, Ph.D., suggests we treat our future self as a member of the family. Think about that for a moment. Some of you are on budgets. I mean the kind where you actually set money aside each month, maybe even in envelopes, for recurring expenses like utilities, clothing, eating out, toiletries, hair and nails. If you set the money aside for you to have those things today, you also need to set the money aside now so you can afford those same things in the future. You have to admit that makes perfect sense!

Some of you are already ahead of me. I hear you. "I've got an IRA. I'm contributing to my company 401(k) plan. I have a Roth IRA." You are already taking money from your current self and setting it aside for your future self. That's good … well sort of. For those of you who responded I already have an IRA and/or I'm contributing to my company 401(k) plan, I strongly recommend you go back and re-read chapters 4 and 5 before you go any further. If you are not completely put off by market volatility, illiquidity, rigid vesting schedules and penalties, have you looked at your fees? The majority of you who own an IRA are invested in mutual funds, ETFs, managed money and/or variable annuities. Total operating expenses on these run from a low of 0.17 basis points to a high of over 4% every year! Don't be fooled and think that you are not paying any fees because you have a "no-load" mutual fund. There are no free lunches. Do you work for free? I didn't think so. Neither do fund/money managers.

The 401(k) plan is no different. If you are miffed about paying 1-2% on your managed money account wait until you look under the hood of your 401(k) plan. I read recently that if you work for a big company the average 401(k) costs approximately 3.7% annually and that it's a little higher for smaller companies. Let me put that into perspective for you. If your 401(k) assets earn 3.7% this year, you will receive zero, nothing, nada! That 3.7% return goes straight to the plan administrator. Do not pass Go. Do not collect $200. That is absolute madness! Since January 1, 1929 the S&P500 has risen at a 9.4% annualized rate, according to the data from Ibbotson

Associates, assuming dividends were reinvested. I point this out because 3.7% is equal to 40% of the market's historical average return AND THEY HAVE NO RISK meaning they are going to get their 3.7% from your return or your principal. It matters not to them. That is one heck of a deal for the plan administrator! Let me be even more clear. If the market is flat and your 401(k) doesn't earn a return in a particular year…your actual return is "negative" 3.7%. Yep! Those fees come out whether you earn them or not. This makes me crazy just thinking about it. And yes, if the market causes your 401(k) to lose 10%…c'mon you can do the math…10 + 3.7 = (13.7%). For those of you who aren't familiar with general ledger entries, that is a 13.7% LOSS in your 401(k). Are you upset yet? You should be!

For those of you who are reading this book thinking, "I've got this fee thing under control, I'm invested in the Vanguard 500 Index Fund," let me remind you that that fund by design is built to replicate the performance of the S&P 500 Index. Last I checked, that index went up AND down. You might have a handle on the fees but you have absolutely NO protection whatsoever from market volatility.

Before I move into my next rant, I feel the need to warn you. You may have noticed that my tone is strengthening. I have uncovered and shared with you some very inconvenient truths. You should be good and irritated by now. I know I am! I suppose you could sit there and do nothing but I'd rather you get fired up and do SOMETHING! The sole purpose behind me writing this book is to motivate you to take action. I believe I speak for more than a few of you when I say, "you have a mess on your hands!" It's time to take control of YOUR retirement. It's your money. Not theirs! You have a choice. It might not be the most "popular" thing to do but that doesn't mean it's the wrong thing to do and that it won't work. What it typically means is that it requires a little bit of effort on your part and since most people would rather sit in a drive-thru that is wrapped around the building twice rather than park and go inside, I'm guessing I've got my work cut out for me!

Does everyone remember what tax-deferral is and why it is a bad, a very bad, thing? Tax-deferral is exactly what it says it is. You pay your income tax later. The bait to entice you into this sticky, suffocating web is that you will "supposedly" be in a lower tax bracket in retirement than you are while working. We've already busted this myth. To reach your retirement goal of maintaining your lifestyle you will actually have to make more money in retirement than while working due to the effect of inflation and higher taxes. So by deferring taxes you are actually creating a BIGGER problem for yourself. Think about it like this. Every time you invest a dollar into a tax-deferred account [IRA, 401(k), 403(b), annuity, deferred compensation plan, etc.], you are attaching a blank check payable to the IRS and signed by you. The amount, however, is conveniently (for the government, not you) left blank. You see, you have NO idea what tax bracket you will be in when you retire and decide to start withdrawing from your tax-deferred account(s). So in essence you are saying to the IRS, "whenever you decide how much tax I owe on that dollar let me know and I'll fill it in". And if that's not bad enough, every dollar that your dollar makes ALSO has a blank check attached to IT! People wake up!! We are staring at nearly $18 trillion in debt. Don't think for one minute that the IRS is going to be easy on you. If you want to protect your Future Self from higher income taxes, STOP DEFERRING YOUR INCOME TAX. RIGHT NOW! It's as simple as that. You know exactly what your income tax liability is today. PAY IT. Whatever you have leftover is yours to invest any way you see fit.

I know some of you reading this book have never seen a paper check and probably squinted just a little bit when you read that last paragraph. But some of you still write checks to this day and know exactly what I am talking about. Let me ask you this. Have you ever lost a check? You are looking through your ledger ... 4682 to the utility company ... 4683 to the grocery store, 4685 to the lawn boy ... oh, my gosh! Where is check 4684? It's not in my checkbook. Where could it be? Have I lost it? Did someone steal it? I need to call the bank right now and put a stop payment on that check before someone finds it and tries to cash it! And God forbid you lose an entire book of checks! Now let me ask you this. How many of you would like to put stop payments on all those blank checks you have written to the IRS? Me, me, me, me, me!!!! Well all right then. It is time to stand up, stretch and freshen up your cup of Joe because I'm about to teach you how to defuse a ticking tax bomb.

I renamed all tax-deferred accounts "ticking tax bombs" about 3 years ago. I mean think about it. The more taxes you defer the more the pressure builds. When you hit retirement in 10, 20 or 30 years, that thing is going to blow sky high doing some major damage to your retirement. Heck, it could destroy your retirement all together! Remember the dominos?

It seems the most popular video games these days involve warfare. So I've borrowed a "cheat code" for defusing a bomb.

Defuse Bomb

You are surrounded by 50-gallon steel drums full of highly explosive toxic waste, and facing a bomb that reads 2 minutes until detonation. Your aim is to disable the bomb. There are 3 unlabeled wires that must be cut in the correct sequence in order to interrupt detonation. You must first cut the wire that leads to the Primer, followed by the Reactor wire, and finally the wire that feeds the Ignition Timer. You are equipped with a pair of wire cutters and a splicer. Be careful, as clipping the wrong wire accelerates the detonation time. Remain calm and don't let the pressure impair your judgment. The fate of the world is in your hands. Good luck!

With your Future Self in mind, you must cut off the "Primer" to your tax-deferred account(s). STOP CONTRIBUTING TO TAX-DEFERRED ACCOUNTS IMMEDIATELY. Stop priming these deadly financial devices! The closer you get to retirement the shorter the fuse. So stomp out the fuse NOW while there is still time to disarm this mess. Call your HR Manager, or better yet go online and change your future 401(k) contributions to zero, nothing, nada. And please don't whine about losing the matching contribution. Re-read the cheat code. Remain calm and don't let the pressure impair your judgment. We have already learned it is NOT free money. It is VERY EXPENSIVE money. If your colleagues think you're crazy then so be it. They will understand completely once they retire, but by then it will be too late.

Don't forget about your traditional IRAs and deferred compensation plans. Do NOT contribute one more dollar to a plan that has a blank check attached to it. I don't care what your CPA or accountant says next April about how much money you can save on your taxes by adding $5500 to your IRA or $25,000 to SEP plan. DON'T DO IT! Instead, give them a copy of this book! In order to cut the primer to your ticking tax bomb, you must stop ALL contributions indefinitely.

We are now surrounded by 50-gallon steel drums full of highly explosive toxic waste, aka our tax-deferred accounts. I consider them toxic because they are filled with market risks, high fees, penalties and taxes…can't you just picture green slime everywhere? Time is ticking people. There is no time to waste! The cheat code tells us the next wire to cut is the Reactor Wire. OK. You have stopped adding new funds to your tax-deferred account(s). Is there anything you can do with the money that is already in there to help improve your situation? Yes. As a matter of fact, there is. If you have a traditional IRA, you may want to consider an Indexed Annuity. You will recall in Chapter 8 "Annuities Are Not Bad Investments," with an indexed annuity if the market goes up, your account value goes up. If the market goes down, you can't lose. These annuities consider the performance of a stock index such as the S&P 500 to determine how much your account is credited at the end of the term. Since the money is never invested in the stock market, the account value will never go down due to market volatility. In years where the S&P 500 loses money, the account is credited with zero. This alternative not only removes market risk from the monies sitting in your IRA but it also has the potential to reduce your fees. Currently there is a VERY attractive indexed annuity with an income rider that is 95 basis points, all in. That is less than 1% per year. I guarantee you are paying more than that right now and you have absolutely no guarantees. That's a toxic situation!

What about the monies in the 401(k)? How can we reposition those dollars to make them less toxic? As I am sure you have already gathered, indexed annuities are not an option within your 401(k). However, most 401(k) plans now offer index funds as a sub-account. PLEASE DO NOT MISUNDERSTAND. An index fund does NOT work like an indexed annuity. In Chapter 10, Do You Understand Indexing, we learned that index funds are built by design to "mirror" a particular index. So while you might think it is admirable to do as well as the S&P500 Index fund, how do you feel when that index loses 10%? Oh, you're not a fan? Well your index fund is a "copy cat" so when the index goes down so does your 401(k) balance. The ONLY redemption in using index funds for your 401(k) monies is that they are pretty darn cheap thus reducing your overall plan costs. Most plans these days also have a fixed account option, which should have lower fees. Be careful with bond funds, as they are not always what they seem. Even government securities funds can lose money. Bottom line, get with a knowledgeable Financial Advisor and review your 401(k) investment options. DON'T ASK YOUR HR MANAGER. They don't know and even if they do, they won't tell you. Why? Because the company won't let them "advise" you. They believe it is a liability…that if the HR Manager recommends where to put your money, you follow their recommendation and ultimately lose money you will sue the company. What a load of crap! They will give you a plan, encourage you to use it by dangling the company match (the VERY expensive money) and lying about being in a lower tax bracket when you retire, but won't help you use it.

We have cut the Primer wire and the Reactor wire. We are no longer contributing to tax-deferred accounts and we have repositioned the assets as best we can to reduce market volatility and fees. All that is left to do is cut the wire that feeds the Ignition Timer. Wipe the sweat from your brow and let's talk about how to manage the taxes that you WILL owe on the monies sitting in your tax-deferred accounts.

Before we move into the last phase of defusing your Ticking Tax Bomb, let me be clear. This is NOT something you should attempt on your own. When the Bomb Squad arrives on the scene and the doors of the van fly open, one guy with a cape does not jump out and say, "let's do this!" No, it's quite the opposite. An entire team of experienced professionals climbs out of those vans, each one with a job to do. This is no different. At the very least, you should be using an educated and experienced Financial Advisor and Accountant or CPA. I hope you also have an attorney on your team and they should know about and work with each other. I fully suspect the majority of you reading his book are DIYers or have been in the past. DIYers? Do-It-Yourself-ers. In several of her books, Suze encourages you to manage your own money in order to save commissions/fees. How's that working out for you? You opened an IRA with your favorite discount brokerage firm and have been throwing money (with blank checks attached to it) into "no-load" mutual funds for years. Market volatility and fees have prevented you from making any "real" money. You can't access your money without penalties and if that's not enough you now owe MORE money in taxes than you would have if you had paid them upfront. That, my friend, is what happens when a plumber tries to wire a house. It burns to the ground!

My initial thoughts to managing the tax you owe on the monies you have in tax-deferred accounts is kind of like removing a sticky band-aid from your hairy arm. Yea, it's gonna hurt like heck so JUST RIP IT OFF ALREADY! I said that was my initial thought, not my final thought. Our goal is to pay as little income tax as possible on this money. We have to take advantage of every possible opportunity to make sure this thing does not explode and spew toxic waste all over your retirement. With that in mind, let's look at the rules to access tax-deferred savings. The rules vary by type of account so for the purpose of this discussion we will talk about a Traditional IRA and 401(k) plan.

To protect and provide for your Future Self you must take control of what you can. Working with professionals, I recommend you begin to bleed your tax-deferred accounts dry. What I mean by that is start withdrawing your money and pay taxes NOW. You do realize that unless your account loses money you will more than likely never owe less tax than you owe today. Your tax liability INCREASES with every dollar you make! Now, I know there are people screaming at the top of their lungs, "if I take money now I'll owe taxes AND a penalty you idiot"! Maybe you will, maybe you won't. AND even if you DO have to pay both it could still wind up being LESS than what you may owe when your ticking tax bomb detonates!

We've all heard of the 59½ and 70½ rules for traditional IRAs. Generally speaking, if you take your money BEFORE age 59½ you will owe a penalty and if you DON'T take some of your money out at age 70½ you will owe a penalty. There is all kind of speculation around how the powers that be came up with 59½ and 70½. I don't make the rules, I just try to bend them! The penalty for taking money prior to age 59½ is 10% unless you meet one of the exceptions to this rule. The exceptions include: death, disability, higher education, buying a home and medical needs. If you qualify under one of these exceptions, that's great. For the purpose of this conversation though, I am going to assume you do not. But, there is another option that could prove beneficial and that is the Rule 72(t). This rule says that if you take equal, periodic payments for five years or until you are age 59½, whichever is longer, you will not owe the 10% penalty.

That's interesting. Imagine working with a professional to determine exactly how much you can begin withdrawing NOW without increasing your current tax bracket? Some of you caught that but others did not so let me say that a different way. If you are single and have $50,000 of taxable income during 2014, you fall into the 25% Federal Income Tax bracket. Guess what? If you are single and have $89,350 of taxable income during 2014, you ALSO fall into the 25% Federal Income Tax bracket! You may be able to withdraw up to $39,350 from your IRA and still only owe 25% tax. And, if you follow Rule 72(t) and take equal, periodic payments for five years or until you are age 59½, whichever is longer, you will avoid the 10% penalty. If you think 25% is high, you might want to Google the history of Federal Income Tax rates. You may be surprised to learn that things can get a whole lot worse than 25%!

Before we move on, some of you have very unique situations. Maybe you lost your job…maybe you have gone back to school… the bottom line is, your income is currently very low or possibly nonexistent. This is a golden opportunity to bleed some money out of a tax-deferred account and control your tax liability. I cannot emphasize enough how important it is to work with a professional on this last step. The purpose of me writing this book is to get you to OPEN YOUR MIND and THINK FOR YOURSELF. Every situation is unique but don't think for one minute you are stuck and have no options. Where there is a will, there is a way! Don't wait for the IRS to tell you how much you owe. Control what you can and that includes managing the tax you owe on your tax-deferred accounts.

So what do you do if you have a 401(k) plan? That depends. Is it from a previous employer; meaning you have changed jobs and left this account behind? How old are you? If you were 55 years or older when you separated from service, you may want to take distributions directly from the 401(k) rather than rolling it to an IRA. Why? Because the IRS has a neat little provision that applies to Qualified Plans like the 401(k) that says the 10% early withdrawal penalty does NOT apply to the employee who separates from service during or after the year the employee reaches age 55. And, that requirement drops to age 50 for public safety employees in governmental defined benefit plans. Wow! Now that's a nice little tool to have in our tool bucket when trying to defuse a ticking tax bomb! For those of you who separated service prior to age 55/50, you may want to consider rolling over your balance in your plan to an IRA and begin systematic withdrawals. Again, EVERY situation is unique so PLEASE work with an educated experienced professional(s) to develop the best strategy for you and your Future Self.

This brings me to those of you who have a 401(k) and are still employed by the company. This is the worst situation to be in as your options are ... well, you don't have any options for bleeding this account until you separate from service. Unless, your Plan allows for "in-service" withdrawals and I am NOT talking about a 401(k) loan. Depending upon what you find in your Summary Plan Description, you may be able to roll over the following to an IRA:

• Your employer contributions including match and profit sharing

• Your personal after-tax contribution

• Your pre-tax contributions when you hit the age of 59½

By getting these assets into your hands you have the ability to lower fees, lower risk and manage your tax due.

Now for those of you who have a 401(k) with your current employer and do NOT have the luxury of in-service withdrawals, we can certainly clip the Primer Wire by stopping all contributions; we can clip the Reactor Wire by repositioning the assets within the plan reducing market risk and lowering cost; but we will not be able to clip the wire that leads to the Ignition Timer until you have separated service. At that time, work with a professional to design a strategy to manage the tax your Future Self owes. Don't wait until the IRS tells you how much they want. Control what you can.

Some of you have breezed over these last few pages. You are sitting there with a smile on your face and a twinkle in your eye. Why? You don't contribute to a Traditional IRA or a 401(k) for that matter. You took the bull by the horns and jumped on the Roth IRA bandwagon in 1998 and haven't looked back. You even bit the bullet paying the tax due on your current IRA and converted it to a Roth IRA. Then in 2006 your employer amended their 401(k) plan document allowing you to elect Roth IRA tax treatment on your future contributions. Woo-hoo! No ticking tax bomb for you! You got this.

Let's talk about Roth IRAs. Roth IRAs have gained popularity in recent years. They've been more popular with younger investors, who tend to be in lower tax brackets. With a Roth IRA, you pay the income tax upfront (you do not attach a blank check payable to the IRS). By doing so your withdrawals are tax-free, so long as the account has been open five years and you are at least 59½ years of age. As good as that sounds, Roth IRAs may not be the answer. I realize this is a rather bold statement. I would like to defend it with a Case Study I completed wherein I have identified six problems inherent to the Roth IRA.

I used a 28-year-old male, non-smoker with current living expenses of $56,500. He has a Roth IRA and contributes the maximum of $5,500 annually. The funding source for the account is a mutual fund. He desires to retire at age 58 and maintain his current lifestyle. Will he reach his goal?

The long-term average for inflation in the United States is 3.33%. Just to maintain his purchasing power, this investor will need $150,952.85 ($56,500 in today's dollars) at age 58. In order to accumulate enough cash to support this withdrawal for life, the client needs to accumulate $3,773,821.25 over the next 30 years. Why? Ask any financial advisor on the street today how much you can safely withdraw during retirement to make sure you don't run out of money and they will tell you 4%. Actually, that number has started to come down due to the volatility in the stock market. However, for the sake of this case study we will stick with 4%. Assuming the contribution limits for the Roth IRA remain at $5,500 per year for those under age 50, this client would only be able to contribute a total of $173,000 prior to his retirement. The chance of $173,000 growing to $3,773,821.25 over 30 years is ZIP and ZERO! We have our first problem. The IRS knows what a good deal this is and they are not going to let you put any "real" money into these plans. Why? They can't collect any revenue. Duh!

My second concern pertains to the income limitations on Roth IRAs. In 2014, contributions for single filers begin to phase out at $114,000 and for joint filers at $181,000. As your earning potential grows, you may find that you are no longer eligible to make contributions to your Roth IRA. It seems like such a "bate and switch" plan to me. Just when you get to a point where you can comfortably save for retirement they say, "Sorry. You are no longer eligible." The Roth IRA has liquidity provisions prior to retirement making this savings vehicle more attractive to young investors. For example, you can withdraw your contributions at ANY time income tax and penalty free. I know several people who have used the Roth IRA as their Emergency Fund. INVESTOR, BEWARE. Yes, you may withdraw your contributions at any time BUT you will never be allowed to "repay" those funds to your Roth IRA. We have our third problem. The Roth IRA has been "pitched" to young investors as a one-stop shop for their investment dollars. Save for retirement, save for college, rainy day fund, etc. You will NEVER reach your retirement goal if you are accessing your contributions and NOT paying them back. P.S. If you converted an IRA to a Roth IRA, the access to your principal is restricted for 5 years with a few exceptions.

Do you remember our little math exercise on market volatility from earlier? Today the market drops 50%. Tomorrow the market gains 50%. The next morning the Wall Street headlines would read something like, "Shew! Dodged a bullet. Market Flat." After all, if the market went down 50% and up 50% the average return would be 0% for that two-day period (+50 -50 = 0/2 = 0). Right? Do the math with me again. Today I have $100 and lose 50%. I have $50 at the end of the day. Tomorrow I gain 50%. I have $75 at the end of day two ($50 x 50% = $25 + $50 = $75). Your investment is NOT flat! You, my friend, are DOWN $25 or 25%! Due to the contribution limits, you can't invest your Roth IRA in a bank CD and expect it to amount to much. To accumulate enough money to impact your retirement, you need growth…and lots of it. This means you are more than likely using mutual funds, stocks, ETFs and other variable investments to reach your goals. As we have learned, variable products do not go straight up and when they go down, they must recover before they can continue to grow. Market volatility WILL hinder the growth of a Roth IRA invested in a variable source. Herein lies the fourth problem with Roth IRAs.

Let's assume for a moment there are no contribution limits and no income limits. How much would you actually need to contribute in order to accumulate $3,773,821; the amount needed to sustain a 4% withdrawal of $150,952 for life? I decided to visit www.bankrate. com one of my favorite resources for financial calculators. Using an average return of 6.5% and adjusting annually for 2.5% inflation, bankrate.com reports that you would need to save $68,822.84 each year.

Wow! $5,500 per month not $5,500 per year! As bad as that is, that's not the worst of it. I know. I know. I just keep spewing toxic waste everywhere but I'm just reporting the facts people. Aren't you tired of being lied to over and over again? I am! Even if you could invest $5,500 per month AND earn 6.5% return, you still will not meet your retirement goal of $3,773,821 unless that 6.5% is a fixed rate. No. www.bankrate.com did not report bad information. They do, however, calculate the future value of money the way Suze and most every other financial advisor does. What I mean by that is they stack 6.5% on top of your previous year's balance each and every year. Do you realize the DANGER in doing that? For this to come to fruition, the market can NEVER have a down day! That's right. Not ONE single negative day. Why? Because when the market goes down, your investments drop into a hole. The bigger that hole, the longer it takes to crawl out of that hole (break even – no growth – good-bye retirement). Roth IRAs invested in a variable source such as a mutual fund, stock or ETF offer NO GUARANTEES; the fifth problem with the Roth IRA. P.S. If you think you will invest your Roth IRA into a fixed investment, like a bond fund or fixed annuity, good luck finding 6.5% and maintaining that for the next 30 years!

The client in my case study desires to retire at age 58. Can a tax-free withdrawal be made from a Roth IRA at age 58? With a few exceptions, the account must be opened for a minimum of 5 years AND the client must be 59½ years of age of older in order to withdraw your earnings tax-free. Although the Roth IRA currently has no requirements to withdraw money at age 70½, as does the Traditional IRA, tax-free withdrawals of earnings are restricted until BOTH requirements have been met rounding out the sixth problem with the Roth IRA.

It should be quite clear that the Roth IRA, as we know it today, will not allow the client to successfully reach his goal of retiring at age 58.

Notice I said, "the Roth IRA as we know it today". You will also recall I have pointed out that an IRA and a 401(k) are made up of laws; laws that can and do change every day.

On June 4, 2014, Forbes published an article titled, "3 Public Policy Changes That Could Ruin Your Retirement Plan." Jamie Hopkins writes: "Have you ever been playing a game with friends when all of the sudden someone changes the rules in the middle of the game? This feels incredibly unfair, but you might have little or no control over its occurrence. Some proposed public policy changes might present a similar unexpected jolt to an established retirement income plan. For years your plan has been designed around the existing legal structure but all of a sudden, the government can and will change the rules. This can completely disrupt a plan, leaving people who felt financially prepared for retirement under the old rules, scurrying around trying to adapt to the new rules. Because you have little direct control over such changes, it is almost impossible to mitigate or transfer this risk completely. Instead, it is important to keep a watchful eye out for potentially disruptive public policy and legal changes."

Here are the three proposals from President Obama's 2015 fiscal year budget that you might want to pay attention to:

RMDs for Roth IRAs

This proposal wants to "harmonize" the required minimum distribution rules forcing RMDs from a Roth IRA once the owner reaches the age of 70½. If passed, this would force you to withdraw monies that you might have earmarked for later years in retirement causing your income to come up considerably short! Needless to say, it is very important to pay close attention to this proposal as you may need to make adjustments to your retirement plan.

Cap on wealth inside an IRA

The government considers $210,000 per year to be a "secure retirement" and thus should be the most income you are allowed to generate from your tax deferred retirement accounts. This proposal would actually cap the combined balance of your tax-deferred accounts — 401(k), 403(b) and IRA — at $3.2 million dollars. This is the lump sum necessary to generate a $210,000 joint annuity with 100 % survivor benefit from age 62 and continuing for life. Granted, this is a substantial amount and would not impact the majority of investors. That being said, this would put serious limitations on those who have grown accustomed to a higher standard of living. High net worth individuals may need to consider an alternative investment vehicle to subsidize their desired retirement income should this proposal become law.

Reduction in Social Security benefits

This should not come as a surprise. In fact, most of you are expecting something like this to happen. The program is grossly underfunded. Increasing taxes, extending full retirement age and reducing benefits would all help to mend the ailing program but the current focus is on reducing benefits. Currently, you are able to defer benefits to age 70 receiving an 8% increase in benefits for every year you wait after you reach full retirement. It's a really good deal. In fact, this is a strategy we often recommend. If this strategy were taken away, retirement plans would need to be reevaluated and the necessary adjustments made in order to manage potential taxes and meet future income needs.

As you can see, changes to public policy can wreak havoc on even your best plans. Often changes come without much warning giving you little time to prepare which is probably exactly how the government wants it! Thus, we have to stay on our toes and when possible take advantage of opportunities where we maintain control of the asset, not the government.

Well now. If you didn't believe ME that laws can and DO change every single day maybe you will believe Jamie Hopkins and/or

Forbes. Here's the bottom line. You need a plan in the event ANY of these three proposed changes are implemented. I do have to disagree with Jamie on one point though. He said, "Because you have little direct control over such changes, it is almost impossible to mitigate or transfer this risk completely." Before I tell you why I disagree with him, I would like to go back to the Roth IRA for just a moment.

Despite all it's problems and potential changes, the Roth IRA certainly has one VERY attractive feature, tax-free income. Granted, you have to pay income tax on the money you contribute to the Roth IRA but that is the LAST time you will ever have to do that provided you play by the rules…and of course they don't change them in the middle of the game! When I think about the option of paying my tax now instead of later, I get REALLY excited. Think about it. You know exactly what your taxes are today…you have control over how much tax you pay by paying it NOW. No more blank checks payable to the IRS. ALL of the growth your contributions earn will be YOURS to keep. None of it will belong to Uncle Sam.

When I was a little girl, I loved to help my dad with our garden. It was hard work. The land had to be tilled, planted, watered, fertilized and harvested. Ah, the harvest. There is absolutely nothing like fresh half-runner green beans, silver queen corn and juicy ripe tomatoes. My mouth is watering just thinking about it! And it all starts with a few tiny seeds. Mind-boggling when you think about it; that something so small could produce something so big. As I write this, I am flying over Indiana. I look out over the acres and acres of land and can't help but think about the farmer. Imagine for a moment you are a farmer. If you had the option of paying income tax on all of the tiny little seeds you planted instead of the thousands of ears of corn and thousands of pounds of soybeans you expect to harvest, would you do it? Of course you would! In a heartbeat! So please tell me why you are throwing money at traditional IRAs, 401(k)s, 403(b)s, deferred compensation plans and every other type of tax-deferred account known to man? When you defer tax you are saying, "I'd rather pay tax on my harvest not my seed"! When you say it like that, it sounds pretty stupid! Why would anyone do this on purpose? I hear some of you saying, "because my _____(fill in the blank … brother-in-law, CPA, neighbor) told me to" while others of you are asking, "how else are we suppose to save for retirement"?

At the beginning of this book, I set out on a mission to bust several financial myths and to learn all I could about the various products and investment strategies available today in order to help you make better choices for you and your family. Knowing what I now know about how the market works, the limitations of certain products and the low cost and tax-efficiency of others, my mission has morphed into launching a Financial Revolution. An opportunity to protect your Future Self from the toxic waste that "traditional" retirement strategies are contaminated with: contribution limits, higher taxes, laws, market risk, illiquid assets, lack of guarantees and penalties. Jamie stated in the article above, "Because you have little direct control over such changes, it is almost impossible to mitigate or transfer this risk completely." I whole-heartedly disagree. You have a choice. No one is holding a gun to your head forcing you to contribute to a 401(k) plan and if they are, get a new job! Make today the LAST day you are going to let "the masses" tell you what to do with your money. Today, you begin to think for yourself.

For 2015 and beyond, we need a retirement strategy that has:
• No contribution limits
• No income limits
• No market risk
• No liquidity restrictions
• No taxes

Does such a thing exist? Yes. Yes it does! It has been available to consumers since 1998 and with the exception of the last couple of years has been widely ignored or criticized. Why would such a viable alternative be ignored or criticized? Both are intentional acts. You cannot ignore something unless you know it exists. So again, why would anyone intentionally ignore or criticize a retirement strategy that has the potential to put our retirements back on track? I believe you can answer that question for yourself. My job is to expose it and bring it into the spotlight.

I stumbled onto this retirement strategy only recently. I wish I had known about it in 1998. Unfortunately, the "financial powers that be" didn't share this. Why? Think about the healthcare industry for a moment. Believe it or not, the healthcare industry makes MORE money by treating your illness than they do by curing your illness. It's sad, but true. At the end of the day it is about the money. Do you think the IRS wants you to know about a retirement strategy that has no contribution limits, no income limits, no market volatility, no liquidity restrictions and particularly no taxes? Absolutely not! Why? Simple. They make MORE money if you defer your taxes than they would if you paid them up front. On top of that, this retirement strategy comes in the form of a contract, not a law, and as such is protected by the U.S. Constitution. Now, what does that mean? That means, try as they may, the IRS CANNOT manipulate this retirement strategy by changing a law when it is in their best interest to do so. No more changing the rules in the middle of the game! You can implement this retirement strategy with 100% confidence. Said differently, because you maintain control over the contract, it is entirely possible to mitigate or transfer your risk completely.

Chapter 15 | The Antidote

an·ti·dote noun: A substance that stops the harmful effects of a poison; something that corrects or improves the bad effects of something else.

A couple of years ago, I found myself at Cleveland Clinic. My dad had been diagnosed with nonalcoholic steatohepatitis. NASH is a common, often "silent" liver disease. It resembles alcoholic liver disease, but occurs in people who drink little or no alcohol. Most people with NASH feel well and are not aware that they have a liver problem. Nevertheless, NASH can be severe and can lead to cirrhosis, in which the liver is permanently damaged and scarred and no longer able to work properly. At 75 years of age, dad was not a candidate for a liver transplant. Instead, we were referred to Cleveland Clinic where the surgeons performed a TIPS (Transjugular Intrahepatic Portosystemic Shunt) procedure to buy us some time. During this procedure, the doctors tunneled through his liver. A stent was then placed in this tunnel to keep the pathway open. Patients who typically need a TIPS have portal hypertension, meaning they have increased pressure in the portal vein system. This pressure buildup can cause blood to flow backward from the liver into the veins of the spleen, stomach, lower esophagus and intestines causing enlarged vessels, bleeding and the accumulation of fluid in the chest or abdomen.

My dad was no exception. He suffered from portal hypertension causing massive amounts of fluid to accumulate in his chest cavity. About every 4 weeks, the doctors removed 11 liters of fluid just so he could breathe. Full of toxins, this fluid would normally pass through the liver where it would be cleansed before being released back into the bloodstream. By placing a stent in the liver, the fluid was able to flow rather than backup solving one problem and creating another. Diverting these fluids through a stent meant they were no longer being cleansed. As a result, the toxins remained in the bloodstream. Although they gave dad medication to combat the toxins, it was simply too late for him. Within a few short weeks, the poison had taken my dad's life.

I realize this is not the most pleasant story to recount but I could not help but think how this disease parallels the financial health of many consumers today. My dad's health didn't fail over night. No. It happened over a period of years. And even though he felt pretty well and saw his doctor regularly there were small, undetected changes taking place. Let me ask you something. When do most people really get serious about their retirement? If I took a poll, I would guess most people would say five to ten years before retirement. There may be a handful of you who would say 15. Guess what? By that time your accounts are already infected. Is there time to fight it? Yes, but the problem is you don't realize you're infected. You actually feel pretty good. The market is up. You're receiving a company match. Life is good, right up until it's not.

My dad wasn't an alcoholic so why did he die from cirrhosis of the liver? Let's just say that maintaining a proper weight was not easy for him. He would go from one extreme to the other weighing 300 pounds one year and 210 the next only to gain most of it back again. The doctors explained that these fluctuations placed additional stress on his internal organs causing them to wear out prematurely. Do you realize that market risk is doing the exact same thing to your retirement accounts? When you lose 50% of $100, how much do you have to earn to get back to $100? 100%.

You see, once you lose 50% you only have $50 to work with. To get back to $100, you would have to earn 100% on $50. How long do you think it would take to earn 100%? What if the market went down again before you made your 100% back? Are you starting to see how market fluctuations are putting stress on your retirement accounts ultimately reducing how long your money will last? Now, take an account that is severely stressed from market fluctuations and poison it with toxic fees, taxes and inflation and you get permanent damage folks. Your retirement account will no longer be able to function properly leaving you with limited options: save more, work longer or live on less. Happy Retirement!

I had lost my dad at the young age of 75. I say young because both of his parents lived into their 90s; he was the youngest of three children and the first of those to pass. What went wrong? Why did he die prematurely? All of the sudden, I wanted to know more about how the body works. I was ashamed at how much I didn't know. After all, this is my body. If I expect to live a long, healthy life then I might want to educate myself on what could get in the way of me actually doing that. What I learned was that everything I put in my mouth eventually passes through my liver where it is cleansed. Wow! The liver is a vital organ. It's easy to think about the heart, the brain and even the lungs as necessary organs to sustain life but somehow the liver had gotten past me. I was busy with life and I simply had not taken the time to educate myself on the fact that the liver removes deadly toxins from the body and without that process the body becomes poisoned and ultimately dies. What an eye-opener! It occurred to me that if I limited my exposure to toxins, my liver would not have to work as hard which should extend it's life, ultimately extending mine. What a concept! I began to educate myself on how our foods are processed and manufactured. I studied side effects of some controversial ingredients that are commonly found in processed foods. I began to read labels for the very first time. I took full responsibility for my body and my health. I decided not to believe everything I hear, see and read. I decided to start asking questions. I changed what I eat and drink, even the chemicals I use around my house. It only makes sense for me to do my part and control what I can control.

The more toxins I can eliminate from my lifestyle, the longer my body should last.

Eliminating toxins. Eureka! I dedicated this book to educating you and opening your eyes to the financial toxins that are poisoning your retirement accounts. Are you listening? Market risk, fees, penalties, taxes and inflation are silent killers. If you do not understand how they work and the potential damage they can do, your money will prematurely run out. It's just that simple. If however, you were to stop dead in your tracks, take full responsibility for your retirement and own every decision you make going forward you might have a fighting chance. You must stop following the crowd! You cannot believe everything you see, hear and read. For the most part, there is always an agenda. Advertising a no-load mutual fund in a financial magazine as "free" is absurd people! Someone has to pay for the ad and I promise you it is not the mutual fund company. They are in business to make money not lose money.

I have been promising you an answer. An antidote, if you will. Defined as a substance that stops the harmful effects of a poison, an antidote is something that corrects or improves the bad effects of something else. So what is it already?

It is indexed universal life insurance.

Yes! That's right. It's LIFE INSURANCE. Indexed universal life, or IUL as it has come to be known, is the most flexible, cost-effective, tax-efficient product available today. Guess what? I don't care if insurance agents make a commission when they sell policies and neither should you! My guess is you don't have a problem paying the mechanic who fixed your car. Your problem lies with the mechanic who fixed your car and replaced six things that were not broken. Does that mean all mechanics are crooks? No! What about tax returns? Do you prefer to pay $49.99 for the latest version of Turbo Tax? Or, have you hired an Accountant or CPA who is worth her weight in gold because she exhausts every possible deduction known to man to reduce your tax liability? I'm guessing the latter.

Every industry is plagued with bad apples. There are tons of financial gurus running around the planet making a killing off of bad advice. Does that mean the financial advisors whose advice actually helps you make more money by avoiding certain pitfalls are unworthy of their pay? Absolutely not!

Let's take a closer look. Indexed universal life has:

• NO contribution limits.
• NO income limits.
• NO market risk.
• NO liquidity restrictions.
• NO taxes if the contracts are structured properly.

This is exactly what we need and anyone can have this plan (even a minor) provided they are insurable or have an insurable-interest. Now, if you are still in agreement with Suze Orman and all of the other talking heads that permanent life insurance is too expensive, go back and reread Chapter 11 – How Much is Too Much? We looked at three case studies: Gen Y, Gen X and a Baby Boomer.

Mr. Gen Y		Mr. Gen X		Mr. Baby Boomer	
Age	Average expenses	Age	Average expenses	Age	Average expenses
65	0.103	65	0.57	75	0.934
95	0.099	95	0.179	95	0.420

Remember Rick Ferri, the author of "The Heavy Toll of Investment Fees" published by Forbes in May 2013, said the average expense ratio for actively managed equity mutual funds is 1.2% and investment grade bond funds have an expense ratio of 0.9%, according to Morningstar. Notice that none of our cases have average expenses of 1.2%. In fact, all of our average expenses are less than the expense ratio of an investment grade bond fund except one and it's not off by much at .934%. Now, can we please shut up about permanent life insurance being expensive? Think for yourself people! Stop believing everything you see, hear and read!!

Moving on to those of you who are screaming, "I don't need life insurance". You might want to rethink that. You are 35 years old, married with two kids, maxing out your 401(k), receiving a $1 for $1 match up to 6% of your pay and also contribute to a Roth IRA on the side. You've run the numbers (which we now know are all wrong unless you are investing in fixed products because you cannot accurately predict the future value of a variable product) and determined that if you maintain your course you will meet your retirement goal. Ok. I'll let you believe that for now. Tomorrow, on your way home from work you are hit and killed by a drunk driver. Who is going to fund your 401(k) and Roth IRA for the next 30 years? Oh, so since you aren't here any more you don't need a retirement plan. Okay, but what about your spouse? How will he take care of your 2 children? Will he have to put them in daycare and find a job to make ends meet? Will they be able to stay in the same home or will they have to move? Will he be able to afford the car payment or will it get repossessed? I can go on and on people. The point is NO ONE is promised tomorrow. An IUL retirement plan has no contribution limits, no income limits, no market risk, no liquidity restrictions, no taxes and it SELF FUNDS. If you do not come home tomorrow, an IUL retirement plan guarantees your family will have the financial resources necessary to maintain their lifestyle. Is the added bonus of a death benefit starting to make more sense to you? For those of you who are closer to retirement, think of the death benefit as a very inexpensive way to leave a legacy. IUL has no market risk ... that means you cannot lose your principal because the market goes down ... and it is cheaper than managed money and the majority of all mutual funds. Indexed universal life is an asset builder and a legacy builder all wrapped up in one!

So what exactly is indexed universal life? It's an index fund on steroids! Seriously though, let's stop and break this thing down. First and foremost, it is a life insurance contract, a universal life insurance contract. What have we learned about this type of insurance policy? In Chapter 9, we learned that universal life insurance combines term life insurance with a savings account. Did you get that? These policies are built on a "term chassis," What do we know about term insurance? IT'S CHEAP! That's right! Term insurance is the cheapest insurance you can buy. But term insurance also has an expiration date, right? Yes and no. Universal Life is designed around one-year renewable term rates. What you need to know is that it has the cheapest rates on the planet, it automatically renews every year and it gets more expensive as we get older. Ah, ha! You said it gets more expensive as we get older. Yes. Yes, I did. Note that the average expenses for our Baby Boomer case study earlier was less than 1%. I said it gets more expensive every year. I did not say it gets more expensive than the alternative every year.

This brings me to the death benefit. How much life insurance do you really need? That's a very good question. The answer depends on what you want to accomplish. Remember IUL is an Asset Builder and a Legacy Builder. Some of you actually completed the Life Insurance Needs Analysis in Chapter 9 because you have small children at home and need to know that if you died prematurely there would be enough coverage to take care of them. Others of you have been salivating as you've read this book and can't wait to use this product as a retirement planning tool. For you, we want to minimize the death benefit, keep the cost as low as possible so that you can maximize accumulation. For you guys, the IRS steps in and says if you want all the perks of indexed universal life insurance — no contribution limits, no income limits, no market risk, no liquidity restrictions, and no taxes — you must have a minimum amount of death benefit. In order to determine the minimum amount of death benefit required, you simply need to know how much you want to save. Your contributions can be made monthly, quarterly, semi-annually or annually. Once issued, each policy has a minimum and maximum premium. You are free to contribute the minimum, the maximum or anything in between. That's the flexible part of the "most flexible, cost-effective, tax-efficient product available today" claim I made earlier. Now, I hear those of you who are screaming that I've said more than once IUL has no contribution limits. I'll say it again. It doesn't. However, in order to maintain the tax-free benefits of the plan, which we will get to shortly, there is a maximum amount of cash allowed per policy. So, if you find yourself in the fantabulous position of wanting to save more than your policy currently allows for, you simply get another policy. Boom!

At this point, we have an inexpensive life insurance policy that you really didn't want to begin with but because it has some really cool features, you've decided to humor me…for now. Thank you. I appreciate that.

So what's all this talk about accumulation? When you contribute more than the minimum premium to your plan, you have an overfunded IUL. Remember the universal life policy combines term insurance with a savings account. The excess premiums are deposited into the savings account portion of the policy. I don't know about your bank, but my bank isn't paying jack-squat on savings accounts. There's nowhere in the world I could retire on what my bank is paying on savings accounts! No worries. This savings account is not your "normal" savings account. As you might expect from the name of the product, the savings account balance receives interest credits based upon an indexing strategy. Note that I did not say ANYTHING about an interest rate. Interest credits and interest rates are two completely different things.

In Chapter 10, I asked the question, "Do You Understand Indexing?" Well, do you? One of the most important things you need to understand about IUL is that you are NEVER invested IN THE MARKET. Wrap your head around that because it is one of the main reasons this strategy outperforms its competition. IUL does NOT attempt to mirror the performance of any index. Rather, it allows policyholders to experience "market-like" returns without ever being invested in the market. How is that even possible? Go back with me one more time to my childhood when my mother took us shopping for school clothes. She used a service called "layaway." I bet you've used it, too. We picked out our clothes, took them to a clerk in the back of the store and paid a small fee which locked-in the price of the clothes for the next 90 days. Now, if my mother decided she did not want the clothes she was not obligated to buy them. She would simply forfeit her small layaway fee. However, if my mom came back to pick up the clothes and there had been a shortage of cotton that summer causing the price of clothes to jump by 20%, the store was obligated to sell her those clothes at the price she had locked-in 90 days before. Did you get that? My mother had the "right" to buy, but was never obligated to buy. The store on the other hand was obligated to sell.

Think about this for a moment. Let's say the S&P 500 is trading today at 1,800. What if you were able to lock-in today's price of the S&P 500 for the next 12 months? For the next year you go about your life, business as usual. Let's say at the end of 12 months, the S&P 500 has increased to 1,980. One hundred and eighty points equates to a 10% gain. Provided the cap on your policy is 10% or greater and you enjoy 100% participation, the savings account portion of your policy will receive a 10% interest credit. 10% return with no market risk. Now that's what I'm talking about!

So what happens when the market goes down? Absolutely nothing! Because your money is never invested in the market, the savings account portion of your contract can never lose money because the market goes down. Granted, in a year where the market does go down and you receive a 0% interest credit the policy expenses will come out causing a decrease in your accumulation value UNLESS you have chosen to place a portion of your policy premiums in the fixed account strategy. What? That's right! These policies offer a fixed strategy in addition to the indexing strategies. Currently, the fixed strategies are paying over 4%. WOW! That's 10 times more than most banks are currently paying on Certificates of Deposit. By working closely with an experienced advisor, you can allocate a portion of your premiums to the fixed account and generate enough interest to cover the policy expenses each year. NICE! So even in a year where the market goes down and the strategy credits 0%, your accumulation value generates enough interest to cover the expenses! Are you getting excited yet? This is good stuff!

No more market risk. Can you believe it? No more wild market fluctuations placing additional stress on retirement accounts causing them to run out of money prematurely. No more stress. Just the peace of mind that comes from knowing your money is safe. Safety. Let's talk about that. How safe is an insurance company? Some of you are frowning right now. You don't like insurance companies. Why? I've heard everything from they're crooks to they have the biggest, tallest most beautifully decorated buildings in New York so they can't possible be good for the consumer. OK. Let me ask you another question. How safe are banks? I suspect most of you just said they are very safe mumbling something under your breath about FDIC insurance. Here's something to think about. The Federal Reserve requires all banks to keep a certain amount of cash reserves on hand. Do you know what that requirement is? It varies from one institution to the next but is approximately 8-10%. Do you know there is a similar requirement for insurance companies? So if banks are considered very safe and keep 8-10% cash reserve on hand, how much would you expect an insurance company to keep on hand? 5%? 10%? 20%? The minimum requirement is 100%. Good insurance companies keep 105-120% in reserve. Let me say that again. Insurance companies keep anywhere from 100-120% cash reserves on hand. That being said, if you feel comfortable with your local FDIC insured bank, you should feel extremely comfortable with an insurance company! By the way, you do know what FDIC stands for, right? It's the Federal Deposit Insurance Corporation. Oh my! Now that's awkward.

Before we move on to the tax efficiency of IULs, I hope you are curious about the historical performance of an index strategy. I mean, how well can we really do without being invested in the market? It's important to note here that there is more than one index strategy. In fact, there are several strategies available today and more developing. There are strategies based on the S&P 500 index. There are strategies based on international indexes AND there are now blended strategies that remind me of balanced allocation funds. Currently, the most popular strategy is the S&P

500 1-Year Point-to-Point. This strategy records the level of the
index on the day your premium is received and then again one
year later. Any gains are then credited to your policy based upon
your cap and participation rates. The historical performance of any
strategy then is based upon the cap and participation rates of the
policy. For example, if your policy has a 13% cap rate and a 100%
participation rate, the 25-year historical average of the S&P 500
1-Year Point-to-Point strategy is 8.05%. Here's what that means.
If you had had a policy for the last 25 years with a 13% cap rate
and a 100% participation rate, based upon the performance of the
S&P 500 you would have received an average annual interest credit
of 8.05%. Wow! No market risk and 8.05% annually? Where do I
sign?

I know what you're thinking. How long can a 13% cap rate really
last? Cap rates can change annually. You also have the ability to
change how your premium dollars are allocated to the various
indexing strategies annually including the fixed strategy mentioned
earlier. I want to drive home a couple of things before I leave this
topic. Interest rates are at, or near, all time lows. When fixed rates
start to climb, if you are more comfortable receiving a guaranteed
5% or 6% then go for it. Also know this. If cap rates dropped from
13% to 8% tomorrow and the S&P 500 gained 8% you still receive
an 8% interest credit. Don't decide which product you want to
use based upon cap rates alone. Understand that if your policy
has a 13% cap and your neighbor's policy has a 14% cap and the
index gains 13% you both will receive a 13% interest credit. Your
neighbor's performance will only beat yours in years the index
returns more than 13%, which is not that often.

C'mon guys! If you are not about to jump out of your seats, there
is something wrong with you.

One of the BIG things this book tackled is just how toxic tax-
deferral truly is. To claim that it will save you money is one of the
dumbest things I've ever heard and frankly, I'm ashamed that I ever
endorsed it. From now on we must control what we can control
and that includes paying taxes NOW, on the seed, not later when

that seed has grown into a giant apple tree. We know exactly what tax bracket we are in today. We have no idea what tax rates will be in the future although I can almost guarantee you they will be higher than they are today. How foolish it is to hand the IRS a blank check, which is exactly what you do every time you contribute money to a tax-deferred account. Oh and don't forget when they cash those blank checks the amount will include tax on the money you contributed and all the money that money made over the years. Uggghhhh! Makes me sick just thinking about it.

So exactly how does IUL manage to give the IRS the slip? It's quite simple actually. There are only four ways to get money: a gift; you can steal it; you can earn it; or you can borrow it. For the purpose of this conversation, I am going to assume you do not steal it and it is not given to you. That leaves us with either earning it or borrowing it. We know how the IRS taxes money we earn but have you given much thought to how the IRS taxes money you borrow? No. That is not a trick question. You haven't thought about how the IRS taxes money that you borrow because the IRS doesn't tax money that you borrow! Isn't that interesting. So as long as interest is charged on the outstanding balance and the balance has to be repaid at some point in the future, it is by definition "a loan" and as such does not qualify as taxable income. So then, if you could pledge the cash value in your IUL policy as collateral and "borrow" your income during retirement you could avoid paying income tax on all your retirement income. Right? YES! YES! and YES! That is exactly what happens anytime you request money from the cash value or saving account portion of your policy. A loan is created. Interest accrues and it must be paid back. You will either make payments back to yourself/policy during your life OR when you die the loan balance will be netted from the death benefit before it is paid to your beneficiaries. Now, are any other light bulbs starting to flicker? When can you access the cash value inside your IUL? Do you have to be 59 ½ or older and if not will you pay a 10% penalty for accessing your cash early? Uhhhhmmmm .... no! It is YOUR MONEY. If you have the ability to accumulate enough money in your IUL to support your retirement at age 45, then go for it! This is not an IRA, traditional or Roth. This is not a tax-deferred annuity. The IRS has no control over WHEN you take your money. They cannot assess an early withdrawal penalty because it's "a loan" and as such is not even considered taxable income, which means no income tax either.

Let's spend some time discussing exactly "how" you access your cash value or savings account portion of your policy at any time. I think the best way to explain this is with a comparison. How do you withdraw money from your 401(k) or IRA? What we know about tax-deferred accounts is that, well, they are taxable when withdrawn. So if you withdrawal $50,000 from your 401(k) and you are in the 20% tax bracket you actually have $40,000 to live on — OUCH! We also know that in order to get that $50,000 it must be "liquidated". That may seem obvious to you but we need to spend a moment here. Ask any financial advisor what percentage is safe to withdraw during retirement to insure your money lasts a lifetime and the majority of them will reply, 4%. Do a little math and you will discover that for a tax-deferred account to support a $50,000 annual withdraw for life you need an approximate balance of $1,250,000 in your tax-deferred account. Yea, good luck with that one. For the sake of argument, we will assume you were successful and have accumulated $1,250,000. After year one, how much money do you have left? Answer: $1,200,000. Some of you are screaming, "Wait a minute! Hold on! My balance will be more than $1,200,000 because it will still be growing in the market." Will it? What if the market is flat? What if the market goes down? Do you realize I don't have the answer and neither do you so why worry about it? What I do know is that with IUL I can't lose money when the market goes down and if I am borrowing my retirement income ALL my money ($1,250,000) is still earning interest credits, not just the $1,200,000 that would be leftover after taking $50,000 from a 401(k). It is worth noting here that after the market pullback in 2008, the percentage that is safe to withdraw during retirement to insure your money lasts a lifetime has been adjusted to 2.8%. Let me say that differently. If you desire $50,000 of income during retirement you will need to accumulate $1,785,714. How is tax-deferral and market risk working out for you?

Ok, so we borrow our retirement income and all future interest credits will be applied to our entire cash value. Why is that such a big deal? I'm so glad you asked! We need to go back to Chapter 12 where we learned about arbitrage. In economics and finance, arbitrage is the practice of taking advantage of a price difference between two or more markets to capitalize on the imbalance. Have you ever known someone to finance a major purchase when they could have paid cash? Yes. If you're a savvy investor, perhaps you have purchased stocks on margin. Under what circumstances would this be considered a smart move? When money is cheap. In other words, when the interest you are paying on a loan is less than the interest you are earning on your investment, you should consider holding on to your cash and using the bank's money or in this case, the insurance carrier's money. I dare say the majority of people reading this book have purchased an item with a credit card. Some of you may have done so because you didn't have the money to pay for it. Others of you had the money to pay cash but decided to use the store credit card. Why, because they were running a 6 months "same as cash" special. Why pull money out of your savings account or your mutual fund now when you can leave it in there for 6 more months and make some more money? I couldn't agree more provided you have the discipline to pay off the balance in 6 months. This is just one of many examples of how we as consumers use arbitrage in our daily lives. You may not have known it was called arbitrage but that doesn't change the fact that you clearly understand how taking advantage of prices differences can save/ make you money.

Hopefully, you are somewhat intrigued with the idea of borrowing your retirement income. I mean you borrow money for everything else in life … cars, homes, boats, clothes, jewelry…I don't know why you wouldn't consider borrowing your retirement income, especially if you don't have to pay it back until you are dead! Some of you are very intrigued and want to know what type of interest you can expect to pay on these "retirement income loans". Great question. Most policies offer fixed and variable loans and some will let you switch back and worth. Please, please, please do NOT get hung up on a fixed loan. They may be great for a 20-year mortgage but there is a better option when it comes to creating positive arbitrage. I just said positive arbitrage which implies negative arbitrage exist. It does. Negative arbitrage means the interest rate you pay on the loan is more than the interest being credited to your cash value. The loan is costing you money. That's not a good deal and needs to be avoided whenever possible. In order for your IUL Retirement Plan to work at maximum efficiency, we need to experience positive arbitrage as much as possible. A fixed loan is also known as a "wash loan". It's simple. Whatever rate your cash value is credited is the same rate charged on your outstanding loan balance. For example, you receive a 6% interest credit on $1,000,000 and pay 6% interest on the $100,000 you borrowed. That means your $100,000 did not make any money. The fixed loan "washes away" any gains on the portion of your cash value that is pledged as collateral for your outstanding loan balance. Not a very good deal. You didn't lose any money but you also didn't make any money. Consider a variable loan. Currently charging a little over 4%, these loans allow you to make money on the portion of your cash value that is pledged as collateral. Take the example we used earlier. $1,000,000 is credited with 6% including the $100,000 that is pledged as collateral but the loan was only charged 4.3%. The $100,000 pledged as collateral grew by a net 1.7%. What if we received an interest credit closer to the 25-year historical average of 8%? The $100,000 would grow by a net 3.7%. Pretty neat don't you think? Are you starting to understand how annihilating taxes, avoiding market risk and borrowing your retirement income could extend the life of your retirement accounts? Talk about an antidote!

I mentioned earlier that we need to avoid negative arbitrage whenever possible. Remember, negative arbitrage is when the loan is charging more than your cash value is being credited. For example, the market gains 2% and your variable loan charges 4.3%. In this example you would lose 2.3% on the portion of your cash that is pledged as collateral for your loan. Is there a way to avoid negative arbitrage? I believe there is. It may not be 100% fool proof but it is much better than doing nothing at all. By working with an experienced IUL advisor, you can switch from a variable loan to a fixed loan if the two of you have reason to believe the market will return less than the variable loan rate. If you switch to a fixed loan and the market gains 2% what rate will your loan be charged that year? Remember, a fixed loan "washes away" all gains. In this example, your loan would be charged 2% interest. What we have avoided is a 2.3% loss that year on the portion of your account that is pledged as collateral. Nice! Once you and your Experienced IUL Advisor believe the market is positioned to outperform the variable loan rate again, putting you back into a positive arbitrage position, you can switch back. It is important to work with an Experience IUL Advisor because not all policies are created equal. Some only have one type of loan, others may not allow you to switch back and forth and still others may limit how often you can switch back and worth. An Experienced IUL advisor will know the ins and outs of the most competitive policies and how to execute them to allow your IUL retirement plan to function at maximum efficiency.

Let's spend a moment on paying back your loan or loans. Yes, some policies allow you to have more than one loan at the same time. The obvious pay back comes at death. If there is an outstanding loan balance at your death, the balance is netted from the death benefit before it is paid to your beneficiary(s). You're gone. You don't care. But what if you decide to borrow some of your cash value to send a child to college (yes, you can do that). When would that need to be paid back? I'll answer that two ways. The first answer is at death. No different than before. But here is what happens if you get a loan prior to retirement and don't pay it back. When you meet with you experienced IUL advisor, you will determine how much you need to save in order to meet your retirement income goals. If you borrow some of that money prior to retirement and don't pay it back before you retire, then you will receive reduced income during retirement. Note: you cannot borrow all of your policy's cash value. If you were to do so, there would be no monies available to cover policy expenses resulting in the lapse of your policy. This would be devastating to your IUL retirement plan. If your policy were to lapse you would lose your tax-free loan status. Taxes would come due immediately on every penny you have ever borrowed from your policy. So again, I highly recommend working with one of our experienced IUL advisors to insure you avoid costly mistakes such as this.

The second answer is to pay your loan back with interest prior to retirement. Just like you would make a student loan payment to Sallie Mae, you contribute your payments to your policy. As long as your loan is paid-in-full before retirement, your retirement income will be unaffected. I don't care if you pay the balance off the day before you retire. As long as you repaid the principal with interest, your retirement income will be unaffected. Understand, if your original income projection assumed a growth rate of 8.5% and you haven't received 8.5% every year you will not receive the income you were expecting whether you pay the earlier loan off or not. Again, please be sure to work with one of our Experienced IUL advisors from the very beginning. Agents can make an income projection say just about anything they want it to say in order to get your business. I would much rather you underestimate your retirement income and receive a pleasant surprise at retirement than overestimate your retirement income only to discover you can't afford to retire and are now faced with working longer or living on less.

Some of you are thinking IUL is just too good to be true. If it's so good then why hasn't anyone else told me about it or why isn't everyone doing it? Well for starters you have financial celebrities everywhere you turn who fill your heads with bad information. You have accountants, CPAs and HR directors cramming tax-deferral down your throat. Let me ask you one final question. When you invest money, what is your goal? I know the answer.

I know because all of you say the exact same thing. You want to make as much money possible with the least amount of risk. Am I right? Of course I am right! I give to you, indexed universal life. The product that delivers maximum return with minimum risk. I would also like to take this opportunity and remind you of Warren Buffet's two rules of investing:

   1) Never lose money.

   2) Never forget Rule #1

SUMMARY

Chapter 16: The "Miller Family"
(The following is a hypothethical situation)

Rick and Sherry Miller live in Small Town, USA. They were childhood friends and later became high-school sweethearts. Rick's family owned and farmed quite a bit of land. Everyday after school and sometimes even before school, Rick and his brother did what they could to help out. Like many young boys, Rick was enamored with engines. He wanted to know everything there was to know about them. So much so that, at the age of 14, he completely disassembled the one in his dad's 1950 Chevy Truck. His dad had bought it used when Rick was 5. Rick loved that truck. He went everywhere with his dad in it until the day it stopped running. There wasn't any money in the budget to fix an old truck, so it sat in the barn.

School was out for the summer, and every time Rick passed the barn he caught himself looking at that old truck. One morning, with the help of his brother, he completely disassembled the engine. This soon-to-be high school sophomore, equipped with nothing more than ingenuity and a few spare parts, reassembled that engine. Guess what? It started!

As soon as Sherry graduated high school and turned 18, they married. The next couple of years weren't easy. Rick was working at a local garage and as a carryout, all while taking night classes at the vocational school. Sherry cleaned houses and did odd jobs here and there to help out as much as she could but soon realized she was pregnant with their first child. Their first child turned out to be twin boys, Billy and Mark. Before long, Rick had finished his night classes and become a certified diesel mechanic. He went full-time at the local garage and received a raise, which they would need since Sherry was now expecting their third child. A beautiful baby girl named Sarah was born in 1982.

Rick loved working on cars, trucks, tractors. You name it, Rick could fix it! He had been full-time at the garage 10 years when the owner pulled him aside to tell him he was retiring in three years. Jim and his wife had no children and had treated Rick like a son since his first day at the garage. For this reason, they wanted Rick to have it. He was beyond excited! He had always wanted his own garage, his own business. Rick was not only a hard worker but was also good with money and had managed to save $20,000. He knew this wasn't even close to what he would need to purchase the garage but he had three years to figure it out. He said, "Yes!"

Rick's mother had succumbed to cancer not long after Sarah was born. His dad continued to run the family farm. One afternoon in the summer of 1992, the phone rang. It was Rick's brother. Their dad had suffered a severe heart attack and would not live through the night. They were devastated. He was only 57!

Rick and his brother now had the responsibility of settling their dad's estate. What they learned in the process was nearly as devastating as the passing of their father. Neither of them had pursued life on the farm, but both wanted to keep the property in the family. So they sold the equipment and had the 600 acres appraised. They were surprised to learn that although their dad was "cash poor," his estate was valued at just over $2 million. What they learned next was that they had nine months to pay Uncle Sam $770,000. What? Why? No! Rick was a mechanic and his brother had become a veterinarian. Neither of them understood the first thing about estate taxes.

In 1992, the estate tax exemption was $600,000. This meant you owed tax on the portion of your estate in excess of $600,000. In their dad's case, the estate owed tax on $1,400,000. You could have pushed them both over with a feather when the accountant told them the estate tax rate. In 1992, that rate was 55%. 55% of $1.4 million is $770,000, and they had nine months to come up with it. Where were they supposed to get that kind of money?

Veterinarians and mechanics don't make that kind of money and besides, Rick was trying to figure out how to buy the garage from Jim. They fretted over it for a bit, but the bottom line was they had no choice but to sell the family farm. A friend of the family listed the property, and Rick and his brother went back to their daily lives.

Three months went by with little to no interest. With only six months until the tax bill was due, they decided to lower the price from the appraised value of $3,000 per acre to $2,500 per acre. Another three months went by, and although a few people had looked at the property, no offers had been made.

With only three months before the tax was due and payable, they lowered the price even further to $2,000 per acre. With only 30 days remaining, they received an offer for $1 million for all 600 acres, including the mineral rights. That was only $1,667 per acre, nearly half of the appraised value. They didn't want to accept the offer, but felt as though they had no choice. They had had one offer in eight months, and although they could get a three-month extension on the tax bill, they feared another offer might not come along within that time frame, or if it did, it might be lower than the offer they had on the table. They sold.

It's important to note here that just because the land sold for $1,667 per acre, it was valued at $3,000 per acre on the date of death. The tax bill of $770,000 stands. Ouch! This is what we refer to in the industry as a "Fire sale." If the truth were known, the buyer more than likely had his eye on the property from day one. He probably understood estate taxes and that the family was strapped for cash. He waited until the 11th hour and made a low-ball offer they simply could not afford to refuse. Sounds horrible I know, but these things happen all the time to people who do not prepare. The sale of the property along with the monies generated from the sale of the equipment totaled $1.2 million. A far cry from the $2 million they thought they had only eight months earlier. After paying Uncle Sam, Rick and his brother split $430,000. What should have been $1 million each, shrunk to $215,000 each.

Rick was not happy, but at least he had the $100,000 he needed to buy the garage from Jim, and he did purchase it. Rick had big plans for the business. He didn't just want to repair engines. He wanted to build them, make them run faster and sell them. This would require more space. So he purchased the adjacent property and built on.

Business was booming. He was doing extremely well. He wanted to save for retirement and help his employees do the same, so with the help of an accountant and one of the accountant's financial advisor buddies, he established one of those 401(k) plans he had heard so much about. He was going to save thousands of dollars by deferring the tax on the money he contributed to the plan and all the money that money made! Rick's tax bracket had started to climb, so he was pretty excited about that.

It was 1999. Rick was 40 years old. The twins had graduated high school. Mark went to work with his dad. Billy, who was not mechanically inclined whatsoever, went to school to become a veterinarian like his uncle. Across town was Smith's Garage, Rick's biggest competitor. He liked Jack Smith. They had graduated together, and Jack had a good head on his shoulders. With Mark now in the business, Rick saw potential for a second location. Rather than start from scratch, he approached Jack with a partnership offer, which he accepted. Things were going very well. The business was growing. The market had exploded, pushing Rick's 401(k) balance over $500,000. Plus he had been able to pay for Billy and Sarah's education and do some additional investing on the side.

He really wanted to open one of those Roth IRAs that had come out a couple years earlier. His taxes were climbing and the thought of receiving tax-free income during retirement made him smile from ear to ear. Unfortunately, Rick and Sherry made too much money and were not eligible to contribute to a Roth IRA.

The year 2001 caught Rick by surprise. The bottom started to fall out of the market and he had a scare with cancer. The good news was that since he had lost his mother to cancer at age 47 and his father to a heart attach at age 57, he saw his doctor on a regular basis. When the tests confirmed that he did, in fact, have cancer, it was in the very early stages. Rick was young and otherwise in good health. His body responded well to the treatments, and within nine months, he was in remission.

Rick did his best to keep up with the business and all his investments while he was sick but it wasn't easy. Mark had stepped up and done a great job, but the market had taken a beating. Rick hadn't heard from his financial advisor in months. When he called to get an update on his accounts, he was told the advisor was no longer with the firm and that his account had been assigned to another advisor; someone he had never even met. He was able to speak with the new advisor, who assured Rick that since his investments were long-term investments, short-term market fluctuations were to be expected but certainly nothing to worry about. In fact, he encouraged Rick to buy more while the market was "on sale," which he did.

Over the next couple of years, the market continued to get hammered. But things weren't all bad. Although the economy was suffering, the one thing Rick had going for him was that people were repairing the vehicles they had instead of spending money on new ones. Sarah graduated from college with a teaching degree and simultaneously announced her engagement to Joe, the love of her life. They were married in the summer of 2003. In 2004, Rick opened a third location, and his first grandchild was born.

The market had finally turned around. His $500,000 401(k) had dropped to $325,000, but it had almost recovered by the end of 2006. The last few years had been difficult, to say the least, but the market seemed to be back on track. In 2007 his balance was $525,000. And then, it wasn't. The housing bubble burst, banks everywhere failed and unemployment soared. Everything went into a tailspin. The bottom fell out of the market for the second time in 10 years, but this time there was nowhere to run. Stocks were down. Bonds were down. Everything was down, including Rick's

401(k). He watched as his balance dropped to $332,000. He was now 49 years old. He had met with the new financial guy a few years before who did a 20-year financial plan for him. Rick's goal was to retire with $1 million when he turned 65. The advisor assured him that he would be able to draw 6% of $1 million when he retired if he continued to save at the rate projected. Rick and Sherry both felt they could live comfortably on $60,000 per year. But here he was four years into the plan doing exactly what the advisor told him to do and his balance was not going up. In fact, he was almost back to the balance he had at the end of 2003! How in the world was he going to afford to retire in 14 years? Rick was a smart guy and knew that he would have to save more, work longer or retire on less. That just didn't seem fair. He had done everything he was told to do: Work hard, save money, invest wisely and don't pay any more income tax than absolutely necessary. Rick told himself that if he ever got back to $500,000 he was finished with the market. Heck, he could open a fourth location and make more money than the stock market!

I met Rick and Sherry in 2011. They came to one of my seminars. The 401(k) balance was finally above $500,000 again and they were desperately looking for answers. During the seminar, I explained how the market truly works. I took a bold stand against 401(k) plans and all other forms of tax-deferral. I explained the hidden fees within various types of investments. I discussed inflation, our country's deficit and the direction I expect taxes to go in the future. I answered questions about Social Security, discussed life expectancy and the need for long-term care. About halfway through the seminar, Sherry raised her hand and asked, "If everything we've been told to do doesn't work, then what are we supposed to do?" I remember telling Sherry that was a great question, and thanked her for asking it.

I began to explain indexed universal life plans. I explained how they are life insurance policies, and they should not fear them. I thoroughly explained the policy expenses and how the plans could be designed with minimum expenses (much less than they are paying for their current investments) and maximum potential for accumulation in order to produce tax-free income during retirement. We talked about indexing strategies and how you can receive "market-like" returns without ever being invested in the market. I explained that the only way to get money out of a 401(k) plan or any other traditional investment was to actually liquidate or "spend down" some of the asset.

It didn't take long for them to realize the money could not possibly last a lifetime. Future market volatility and high expenses added to the fact they now need more to live on than they originally thought because of inflation and higher taxes — which is not what the accountant and his financial advisor buddy said would happen at all when they set up the 401(k) plan.

When the evening came to a close, Sherry was the first one to go to the back of the room to schedule their complimentary consultation. I overheard her say to my scheduler, "first available." I was pleased they wanted to meet with me sooner rather than later, but I saw a look of fear in their face and I felt badly for them.

A couple of days later, Rick and Sherry sat in my office telling me their story much as I have recounted to you here. They were high school sweethearts who had been married for 32 years. They had three children and two grandchildren. Mark had followed in his dad's footsteps and was making a significant contribution to the business, while Billy had gone the route of a veterinarian and Sarah, mother of two, had become a high school science teacher. The business had one partner and no debt. Their investments included a 401(k), variable annuity and some mutual funds. They had no long-term care insurance and above all they did NOT want their kids to go through what Rick and his brother had gone through with their dad's estate tax fiasco.

Rick and Sherry were very curious about indexed universal life plans. They asked me to explain how their money could go up when the market went up but not lose when the market went down. I asked them to imagine the S&P 500 was trading at 1,000 today — it's not, but it makes the math easy! Using the analogy of layaway, we would hypothetically put the index in layaway by paying a small layaway fee to lock in today's price of 1,000 for the next 12 months. This is exactly what buying an "option" on the index does. Over the next 12 months, we go about life as usual. The market will go up, down and sideways, but we really don't care because our money is not invested in the market. The insurance company holds your money in a separate account until the one-year anniversary of your policy. When that day comes, they look at the value of the index to determine how much, if any, you will receive as an interest credit. Let's assume the index was valued at 1,100 after 12 months, an increase of 100 points or 10%. If your policy had a 10% or higher cap and a 100% participation rate, your policy would receive a 10% interest credit. How? You ask. Think of it like this. If you knew you could buy something for $1,000 and were guaranteed someone would buy it from you today for $1,100, you would buy it in a heartbeat and sell it to that person immediately. The insurance company owns the option on the index that gives them the right, but not the obligation, to do just that! If Rick had $500,000 in an IUL instead of his 401(k), $50,000 would be credited to his cash value and he was never invested in the market. You might be thinking that in an up year you could do as well as an IUL but you would be wrong. Why? The chances of the market going up 365 days in a row are slim, at best. For Rick's 401(k) to be worth $550,000 in a year where the market went up 10%, the market could never have a down day. Remember, when the market goes down, you not only have to recover what you lost but you have less money to recover with.

The insurance company owns the option on the index that gives them the right but not the obligation. What does "but not the obligation" mean? Take the same example as above but this time let's say after one year the S&P 500 is valued at 900. In this example, the index has dropped 100 points, or lost 10%. Remember, I said you make money when the market goes up, but you can't lose money because the market goes down. Are you interested in cashing in a layaway ticket to purchase something for $1,000 so you

can sell it to someone else for $900 and realize a 10% loss? Uh, no
Of course, you're not! And guess what? Because the option gives
the insurance company the "right" to buy but not the "obligation"
to buy, they don't have to. Viola! Market goes down 10%. You are
not invested in the market to begin with. An IUL plan would hold
steady at $500,000.

I watched Rick and Sherry become both sad and excited at the
same time. They were excited about the future but completely sick
they had not heard about this option years ago.

I asked them to go one step further with me. I wanted to explain
the phrase "lock and reset." Imagine you're sitting outside on
your front porch when your neighbor opens his 401(k) statement
after the market has gone down 10%. (Insert curse words here!)
No doubt he is not happy. He happens to notice that you opened
your statement but didn't have the same reaction. What he doesn't
know is that you have an IUL plan and that instead of waiting
for the market to go from 900 back to 1,000 before you can make
money again — kind of like the decade from 2000-2010 — you
have the option to start making money now. How? Meet "lock and
reset." Every year on your policy anniversary, you put the index on
"layaway" again. In this particular example, the insurance company
is going to purchase an option on the S&P 500 at 900. At the end of
one year, if the market is back to 1,000, you, my friend, will receive
an 11% interest credit if your policy has an 11% or higher cap. Rick
spoke up and said, "You mean a 10% credit right"? I replied, "No. I
mean an 11% credit,"

$$100/900 \times 100\% = 11\%$$

I asked them how they thought their neighbor's 401(k) would do
in this example. They said "probably about the same." Nope. Why?
Because they lost 10% the year before, they now have less money
to recover with. Rick and Sherry were starting to realize that they
didn't need to take risks in the market to grow their money.

Before leaving this part of the conversation, I made sure Rick and Sherry understood these policies have fixed interest rate options in addition to the index strategies. So if we believe the market is going to stay in negative territory for a prolonged period of time, we can switch our strategy allocation to the fixed option and receive interest while we wait for the market to turn around. Options. I love options!

Rick looked at me and said, "Can I shut down the company 401(k) plan?" He was sick that he had gone down the wrong path all these years and felt responsible for encouraging his employees to do the same.

The next week I met with Rick and Sherry and proposed the strategy on the next page.

Rick and Sherry had no problem with step 1. In fact they had stopped their 401(k) contributions before they came back for their second appointment.

Step 2 was to transfer the $95,000 variable annuity, which was loaded with fees and exposed to market risk, into an indexed annuity. Although the income generated from this investment would be taxable when withdrawn, an indexed annuity would protect the asset from future market risk and lower the expenses.

The thought of saving money and protecting their principal was music to their ears.

Next, I had taken the current balance of the 401(k) along with the value of the new indexed annuity and projected them into the future eight years using a modest rate of 4%. I explained to Rick and Sherry that you could not accurately project the future value of a variable product but that projections involving fixed products were much more accurate since they could not lose money when the market went down. $600,000 averaging 4% over the next eight years would grow to $ 821,141. Rick and Sherry had their eyes set on retiring at age 65. My recommendation had them retiring at age 60, five years early. We would need $76,006 per year, which is the $60,000 Rick and Sherry desired, adjusted for 3% inflation

Miller Family Proposal

1) *Stop all funding to tax-deferred accounts immediately: 401(k), variable annuity.*

2) *Reallocate tax-deferred assets to index products to protect them from future market risk.*

3) *Estimate the future tax liability of all tax-deferred accounts. Establish an IUL plan to pay future taxes.*

4) *Redirect contributions for both Rick and Sherry into an IUL retirement plan to generate tax-free income for their retirement.*

5) *Terminate the company 401(k). Hold a staff meeting to educate the employees on the IUL option. Offer to match their contributions into these new plans.*

6) *Meet with a local attorney to draw up a buy-sell agreement to protect Sherry and Mark upon Rick's death.*

7) *Purchase a second-to-die life insurance policy that would pay to Billy and Sarah after both Rick and Sherry passed an amount that would equal the value of Mark's share of the business.*

8) *Establish IUL retirement plans for Mark, Billy and Sarah so they could begin saving for retirement and protect their families from loss of income should they die.*

9) *Establish IUL college plans for Molly and Jacob.*

10) *Meet with an estate planning attorney to establish The Miller Family Living Trust. Value the business along with other assets and determine both current and future estate tax liability, if any.*

Rick Miller   Date

Sherry Miller   Date

Jonda K. Lowe   Date

over the next eight years. Based on current income tax rates, they would owe $7,500 federal income tax. They would have owed more if they lived in a state with state income tax. Since we would need all $76,000 to meet our annual retirement income goal, I recommended we establish a small IUL plan just to pay the taxes on the income received from the tax-deferred accounts. Sherry jumped in and asked, "are you recommending we pay the income tax due with tax-free dollars?" Yes. Yes I was! She had a look of satisfaction on her face like a small piece of justice had been served. Up until last week, Rick had been contributing the max of $16,500 to his 401(k) plan. These dollars would now be redirected to an IUL retirement plan. I explained that since we are dealing with life insurance and want to minimize the expenses within the policy we should consider placing the policy on Sherry. Sherry was two years younger than Rick, and the cost of insurance for a female is cheaper than the cost of insurance for a male the same age. Besides, Rick had had a scare with cancer. It just made sense to go this route and they agreed. My goal with this particular policy was to fund it for eight years and then let it accumulate for another 10. Rick and Sherry would contribute to age 60. Retire. Defer their Social Security benefits to age 70. Spend down the 401(k) and indexed annuity assets from age 60 to age 70. At age 70, they would claim their Social Security benefits and begin receiving tax-free income from their IUL retirement plan.

Rick spoke up and said, "shouldn't we take Social Security as soon as we can get it? After all the fund is going broke!" After we had a little laugh, I explained that I believed Social Security would go through some changes but that the program would still be around when they went to retire. Granted, I don't have a crystal ball but the fact that today nearly 56 million people receive Social Security benefits 70% of which are retired workers and dependents tells me if Social Security goes away, a revolution would break out! I went on to explain that for every year you defer your Social Security benefits you receive an 8% increase until you reach 70 years of age. By waiting until 70 to receive benefits, he would receive the maximum benefit available. There was one more reason I recommended deferring the benefits to age 70. I explained to them that Social Security benefits were subject to taxation. Rick sat up in his chair and said, "You mean I'm going to pay tax on a tax?" I replied, "that's the idea but if we plan correctly you won't fall prey to that tax." I explained that if your combined income exceeds $44,000 then 85% of your Social Security benefit is taxed as ordinary income. Clearly Rick and Sherry's income was more than $44,000. I stopped and reminded them that I had recommended they deplete their 401(k) and annuity assets prior to age 70 and then live on Social Security benefits and tax-free income from the IUL. The strategy behind this portion of the recommendation lies in the definition of combined income. The IRS defines combined income as your adjusted gross income plus any tax-exempt interest plus 50% of your Social Security benefits. I pointed out that at age 70 their adjusted gross income would be zero. With the 401(k) and Annuity asset depleted, the only income they would receive would be Social Security and income from the IUL, which is considered a "loan" and therefore not part of their adjusted gross income. Sherry jumped in and said, "If we take Social Security at age 62 we would pay tax on 85% of what we receive but if we wait to age 70 we get to keep it all?" That is correct. Once again, the look of a small victory came over Sherry's face.

Rick was ahead of me and asked when I wanted to talk with his employees about IUL retirement plans. Terminating the 401(k) plan was not in question. The assets would be distributed to the plan participants. They would have the option of rolling them over, moving them into an IUL Retirement Plan or spending them. Rick and Sherry hoped that they would move them into an IUL retirement plan and even decided to offer matching funds if they did so.

Rick had not been shy about his business continuation plans. Miller's Automotive would stay in the family and pass to Mark. Rick had made that clear to Jack when he negotiated the partnership. Jack and Mary had no children so the only person he was concerned about was Mary if he passed before she did. I recommended they establish a buy-sell entity purchase plan. In an entity purchase plan, also known as a stock redemption plan, the company agrees in advance to buy the interest of a deceased owner while the deceased owner agrees to sell his or her ownership interests to the company. The company applies for and is beneficiary of a life insurance policy on each owner. The business pays the premiums and owns the policies. At death, the company receives the death benefit, which they use to purchase the agreed business interest from the decedent's estate. This recommendation would accomplish three things: Sherry would receive a lump sum at Rick's death to supplement her retirement; Mary would receive a lump sum at Jack's death to supplement her retirement; and Mark would become the sole shareholder. Rick liked it. He liked it a lot!

Now the conversation turned to Billy and Sarah. They were both successful on their own and had no interest in the family business. Still, Rick and Sherry had made it clear they wanted to be fair with the children. I told them about a second-to-die policy that could be used to create an inheritance for Billy and Sarah. Basically, this is one policy on two lives. In fact, one of the two can even be sick or grossly overweight. As long as one is healthy the insurance company will issue the policy since they have no liability when the first person dies. The policy does not pay benefits until both owners are deceased. They were so relieved to hear that something like this existed. They agreed that once the business valuation was completed they would apply for and fund a second-to-die policy for twice the value of the business and appoint Billy and Sarah as equal beneficiaries. I remember the looks on their faces like it was yesterday. The fear and worry was starting to fade. They were beginning to feel good about their future again.

They were not about to leave without finding out exactly what they needed to do to get Billy, Mark and Sarah set up with their own IUL retirement plans. Although each of the kids had started traditional retirement plans, they had not been in them long enough to do much damage. I assured them that we could "diffuse" their ticking tax bombs and get them on the right path while also protecting their families from loss of income due to a premature death. I remember they asked me to open my calendar and wait while they called each one of them on the phone. It was so important for them to make sure the children did not repeat their mistakes. I was happy to wait as each one answered and looked at their calendar to see when it would be convenient for them to come by the office. Sherry was talking with Sarah who was having trouble finding time between teaching and the kid's after-school schedules. She interrupted and said, "I don't care what you have to cancel or reschedule, just be sure to come in next week. This is important and needs to be taken care of now." All three of them were in my office the following week to set up their own IUL retirement plans.

Rick reached for his phone. Instead of making a call, he showed me a picture of Molly and Jacob, Sarah's two children. These were his only grandchildren, his pride and joy. He looked at me and asked, "What are we going to do for these little guys?" Molly was 8 and Jacob was 7. Although Sarah was a high school science teacher, they had not established college funds for either of the children. I asked if they had purchased life insurance for them to which he responded, "No. I wouldn't dream of benefitting from the death of one of our children or grand children." I had heard this objection many times before. I began to tell Rick and Sherry about a lady I had worked with a few years before. Her son was 20 years old and although she and his dad were divorced, they had purchased a $250,000 permanent life insurance policy on him when he was 2 years old. They decided to use the policy as a savings account and "overfund" it for his benefit. When he got ready to go to college, he was able to purchase a used car, his books and a computer all from the cash value of his policy. Not long after his 20th birthday he was diagnosed with Crohn's disease. He was now uninsurable. Had his parents not given him the gift of life insurance at such a young age, he would never have been able to get coverage to protect his future family.

By starting these plans at such a young age the cost of insurance is unbelievably low allowing the cash value to soar. If you start them early enough, you can fund them for 10 years and then let them run. There is money for college, a down payment on a house, retirement, anything you want. It's your money!

I closed the meeting by giving Rick and Sherry the name of an estate planning attorney in town. Rick and his brother had lost a substantial amount of their inheritance to estate tax because their parents did not plan. This would not be the case with Rick and Sherry if I had anything to do with it. I encouraged them to obtain a business valuation in order to accurately assess the present value of the estate. Once the estate had been valued the attorney could determine if there was an estate tax liability based upon current law. He would also meet with them annually to reassess the value of the estate and discuss any changes in the law that would negatively impact their estate. You have to plan to avoid mistakes. It doesn't just happen.

Rick and Sherry were pleased with my recommendation. It addressed all of their concerns and put their retirement plans back on track. In fact, by implementing the changes now they would have the option to retire five years earlier than they had originally planned. I could tell that was a nice surprise.

If Rick and Sherry had never met me, chances are they would have continued down the wrong path. If the market had cooperated and Rick had $1 million in his 401(k) at age 65, he would need to withdrawal $100,000 in year one to meet his retirement income needs. Remember at age 52, Rick and Sherry wanted $60,000 in retirement income. $60,000 adjusted for 3% inflation over 13 years (age 52 to 65) is $88,112. Because all of this money is in tax-deferred plans they would owe $11,638 in federal taxes based upon today's income tax brackets, which we know are going to be higher in the future. So let's review. $100,000 less 11,638 in federal income tax leaves $88,112, which will buy what $60,000 would buy 13 years earlier. At this rate, how long would Rick's 401(k) have lasted? 10 years? 11? On top of that mess if they had claimed their Social

Security benefits at age 65 they would not only have received a lower benefit but they would also have paid income tax on 85% of their benefits. What a nightmare!

Tell me something. Why is it that you will pay $175 for Rock Revival Jeans, $500-plus for an iPhone 6 with a two-year agreement and $45,000 for the new Audi A6 base model? Because you believe it's a fair price for the value received. That's why. Indexed universal life is the most flexible, cost-effective, tax efficient product available today. Don't allow financial celebrities to convince you otherwise.

You should know that on April 14, 2013, Rick and Sherry received the phone call they thought they would never receive. Sarah had been in a fatal car crash. She was just 31 years old. She didn't have the chance to fully fund her retirement plan. She didn't get to see her kids graduate from college. She never met her grandchildren. What she did do was provide her husband with $500,000 in the form of a tax-free death benefit from her IUL plan her parents had been so insistent she setup just a few years earlier. These funds could be used to pay off the mortgage so they could stay in their home, set aside for college educations, retirement or invested to generate immediate income so Joe could stay home and spend time with the children during this very difficult time.

Life Insurance: The gift that keeps on giving.

Getting started

On Feb. 22, 2012, Fox Business published an article titled "(Legally) Cutting Out The Tax Man in Retirement." In it Scott Mann reports, "the life insurance industry has the best IRS-approved retirement savings plan today — and most investors know nothing about it. This retirement savings vehicle is not a company-sponsored, pre-tax qualified, 401(k)-type plan. It's also not a Roth. It's not an annuity or whole life. Despite sales of well over $1 Billion in 2011 for the top 39 carriers surveyed, it is the financial industry's No. 1 secret — indexed universal life (IUL)." With IULs growing in popularity, every Tom, Dick and Harry is jumping on the bandwagon to get their piece of the action. CAUTION: IUL Plans are very powerful but come with moving parts. There are very few insurance salespeople who fully understand IUL and even less who can properly design a plan to put your savings and retirement plans back on track.

You only get one retirement. There are no do-overs!

If you were given this book by an experienced IUL advisor, stop right now and make an appointment with him or her to determine if IUL is right for you. If, however, you found this book on your own or you are an insurance professional or financial advisor who would like to know more about the power of IUL, please contact us at your earliest convenience.

Reach me
Jonda Knows, Inc
(844) 455-6697
info@JondaKnows.com
www.JondaKnows.com

About the Author

Jonda K. Lowe was born Aug. 24, 1966, in Huntington, W.V., to John and Betty McComas. She was raised in a Christian home where she was taught to speak the truth even when it was not the most popular thing to do. Lowe believes she owes much of her success to her parents. At an early age they purchased a toy telephone and encouraged her to practice using it.

During high school, Lowe participated in choir, the debate team and the marching band. The summer before her senior year, she spent 2 weeks in Haiti/Dominican Republic on a mission trip where she gained a sincere appreciation for what she has at home.

Right out of high school, she entered Marshall University. With a love of math and science, she excelled and received a cash award for a paper on fiber optics. Shortly after her first son was born, she graduated with a bachelor of science degree in physics. She began sending resumes with high hopes of working in the research and development department of Ford Motor Co. Her dream of designing a car faded as the call never came. She continued working for a small community bank in Ceredo, W.V., after graduation. Starting out as a part-time teller, she was quickly promoted from one position to the next ultimately landing a full-time position as a personal banker. Lowe recalls the words of Floyd Stark Sr. who said "the client is always right ... without the client we have no reason to unlock our doors each morning." In her role as a personal banker she opened accounts, took loan applications and was over the IRA department. In 1993, the small community bank was sold to a regional bank. In her position, she was asked to project future revenues by applying a new fee schedule to the activities of the current customer base. Lowe recalls sharing with the board her concern for losing customers if the proposed fee schedule were to be implemented. Her concerns were quickly silenced when a board member stated firmly, "if we want clients, we will buy them."

Lowe quickly realized she needed to pursue the next step in

her financial services career. In 1993, she secured a position as a sales assistant for Smith Barney. Working for an adviser who focused on the rollover market, Lowe found her knowledge of IRAs to be quite helpful. Within nine months, she had obtained her securities license. "The more I learned to do, the more he let me do." She noticed during the appointments, the adviser directed his conversation to the husband even though his wife was sitting right beside him. It was at this point, Lowe began to connect with women investors. Shortly after her second son was born, a position opened and she pursued a career as a financial consultant. Although Smith Barney's position was to not promote licensed sales assistants to financial consultants, Lowe's manager who also happened to be a woman took a chance on her telling management, "I will take full responsibility for her."

Over the next 2½ years, Lowe was so successful that Edwards Jones approached her in the fall of 1998 about opening an office for them. With things going so well, she hesitated but ultimately took a leap of faith and opened a new location in South Point, Ohio. Over the next 5½ years, Lowe built her practice one relationship at a time and pioneered the traveling seminar! Her passion for educating women prior to a life-changing event such as death or divorce inspired her to organize a traveling seminar, an opportunity for a female client and one female friend to board a chartered bus and travel to a local attraction for the day. On the two-hour ride to our destination, Lowe taught the women about mutual funds, annuities, tax-free bonds and other investing basics. They spent the day shopping and getting to know each other. It was a win-win for everyone. The women gained valuable information in a fun, comfortable environment and I got to meet new people."

In 2004, Lowe's career led her to West Palm Beach, Fla. She worked briefly for a bond wire house before transitioning to an independent financial advisor. While working for the big wire houses, she was encouraged to recommend their proprietary funds. "I quickly realized that if I did that the company would not only receive the management fee but the fund commission as well," she says. "This is double dipping in my world and I didn't want any part of it. Becoming an independent advisor gave me access to thousands of investment opportunities allowing me to recommend the best solutions for my clients."

Lowe relocated to Jacksonville, Fla., where she lives today, and has continued to challenge traditional thinking and grow her knowledge of the industry. With a goal to always be at the forefront of new developments and ideas, Lowe happened onto a revelation that permanently changed how she coaches her clients into retirement.